ADULT LIFE SKILLS FOR OLDER TEENS

BUDGET, MANAGE MONEY, DISCOVER YOUR CAREER
PATH, ACE COLLEGE AND INTERVIEWS, AND
SUCCEED IN THE WORKPLACE.

MONEY & WORK EDITION
BOOK TWO

KATIE WEBSDELL

Katie Websdell

"Just get a black one with two cup holders!"

CONTENTS

INTRODUCTION

"The two most important days in your life are the day you're born and the day you find out why."

— *MARK TWAIN*

Adulthood was meant to be a utopia. Well, at least it was in my young teenage mind. But it wasn't quite what I expected. Don't get me wrong, being an adult is great. You get to make the rules and are finally in charge of your life - going where and when you want. But that freedom appears to come with endless responsibilities.

We ask, "Why did no one tell me this?" These responsibilities leave us feeling stranded and under the impression that we are adulting wrong when in actual fact, we are not the problem.

You see, school doesn't teach you life. School primarily teaches you how to get through school. A program of required subjects but rarely any addressing life skills. Our families and other adults around us only sometimes equip us with these need-to-know lessons, not because they are setting us up for failure but because these responsibilities have become second nature to them. They forget that it will be brand new to you when you head out into the world by yourself.

But fear not because I am here to help. My name is Katie Websdell, and like every other person who had to inevitably head out into the world, I faced a rude awakening. I did so at a younger-than-average age, and while I fumbled around directionless, I eventually found my feet. I've also watched those I care about struggle, and now that I have children, I want them to avoid facing the same difficulties. Writing this book has come from a place of passion. I wrote this "adult guide" for anyone entering this new and unexplored stage of their lives because most of these difficulties are avoidable.

In the first book of this two-part series, Adult Life Skills for Older Teens: Home Edition, I covered basic living skills that everyone needs to know. In detail, I explored the kitchen with utensils, tools, and tricks everyone could use to thrive independently. I looked at finding your perfect home, cleaning and maintaining it, and all the legal hoo-ha that goes with renting. I looked at security and how you can be more aware and alert. I covered personal care, taking care of your skin, hair, and body, health insurance, and forming safe and healthy relationships. And lastly, I delved into self-love, how important accepting yourself is, and how it helps others see and respect you.

Part of my intention in writing these guides is that I don't want you to make unnecessary mistakes. I will try to teach you from mine. Don't get me wrong, learning from your mistakes is often an excellent way to learn. But some mistakes can be costly and best avoided. Not just in terms of money but in terms of your physical and mental health, education, career, and time. Here are a couple of very different examples.

(a) Imagine getting home and the electricity has been turned off because you forgot to pay, ignored the reminders, or didn't budget sufficient funds to pay your utility bill.

(b) You see a job advertised at a new aeronautics research company near your hometown. You think it sounds exciting. You apply but are unsuccessful even though you have the minimum entry requirements. You don't even get an interview. You find out that the person that got the job was someone you used to know. They didn't seem any more intelligent or different to you. In fact, you knew them well when you were much younger. But you didn't realize that they discovered this was their career path several years ago, and they made plans. They aligned their course subjects to that of this and similar job roles. Out of school, they researched projects, activities, and clubs they could join or participate in related to this field. They spoke with someone in a similar role who told them critical thinking would be a required vital strength. Hence, they honed in on this skill and put it to practice making them excellent problem solvers. For work experience, they interned at a sister company over summer break.

In reality, there may have been a handful of applicants that looked this good on paper for this fantastic role and got interviews. That is often the case for some positions; employers are looking to hire the best candidates. But the secret is you can be one of these few! Think of this as a time machine, and you have the chance to put wheels in motion. I'm giving you the adult cheat sheet and the inside intel.

I will teach you the skills you need in everyday life. Not just skills to get you through but skills to allow you to succeed and thrive. They are skills anyone can learn and will make your life much easier.

Hopefully, you have always had someone there to care for you. But those days are coming to an end. Whether you are actively pursuing your independence or this independence has been thrust onto you. It is time to take on the world all by yourself. Your parents or guardians will remain; they will still help you when needed. But the aim is to show them that you will need their help less and less because you can take care of yourself. You have no idea how happy that will make them. Not just because they will no longer feel like your personal ATM but because they won't have to worry about you as much.

You will face unfamiliar situations at some point in your life. I can't teach you how to avoid all problems, but I can guide you to minimize these occurrences by showing you how to plan ahead. The idea of growing up means one thing: You'll eventually face things that were not part of your original plans. But that doesn't mean you should sit around waiting for trouble to strike; you should take steps to prevent problems from occurring. Even when adulthood comes with unexpected obstacles, it brings plenty of benefits. The good news is that you can prepare yourself for any situation by equipping yourself with skills and knowledge to help you deal with any problems.

WHAT THIS BOOK WILL COVER

I am here with volume two—Adult Life Skills for Older Teens: Money and Work Edition! This book prepares you to enter the job market. Getting your first job and moving out will mean you need to manage money. The reality is that some adults don't even know how to properly manage their funds. No one wants their money to run out too quickly, and budgeting and money management are not skills you immediately grasp and adopt. Yes, it's easy to understand the concept of budgeting, but actually applying it to your life is where the challenges come.

Next, I will look at something that scares even the bravest of the brave—there is nothing worse than driving on your way to college or to work, and something goes wrong with your car. Whether it is unexpected or you see your dashboard light up like a Christmas tree and choose to ignore it, it will always make your heart skip a beat. But car troubles are inevitable because cars don't last forever. Whether you are facing car troubles now or ten years from now, I will impart some knowledge about car maintenance so that you can nip engine burnouts in the bud. I will also help you consider other decisions, such as what to look for in choosing your first car and remembering to add things like oil changes and fuel into your budget.

Beyond book smarts come street smarts. You need to know how to respond in situations where you may not feel safe. You will need to know how to avoid and get out of risky situations and how to help those close to you who may face dangerous situations.

Take guided steps to get to know yourself better, identify your strengths, and discover possible career paths. Learn what sectors and industries may be a fit and what resources are available.

Then, we will look at tips and tricks that will help you academically as you pursue your studies and your academic career. As well as ways to work toward achieving success. This will not give you the answers to all your exams, but it will provide you with the tools you need to acquire and retain the knowledge you study for your exams.

The stress of finding a new job comes in the natural flow of life, after your studies and after you have achieved your qualifications. Whether it is your first job and job interview or you have been working for 10 years and are now seeking new employment. The thought of an interview can be anxiety-inducing. I will help you prepare not just yourself but also your resume or CV for the new venture you are hoping to pursue.

Next, I will impart valuable knowledge to help you become the go-to problem solver. The person who provides answers and solutions to problems rather than adds to the frenzy that problems create. Learning how to solve problems effectively by identifying and addressing the root cause.

Stand out from the competition and learn skills that will boost your employability and make you stand out. Learning and adopting the critical core skills employers are actively looking for. Discover the leader in you and learn to fine-tune those skills to become an effective, authentic leader.

And lastly, on your journey to adulthood, you are also on a journey of self-discovery. The person you are now isn't necessarily the person you will be in the future. We are constantly changing and constantly adapting. This is an integral part of human life. Discovering who you are will help you find your place in this world and what value you bring to it. Discover your core personal values to help guide you through life. I aim to help you find who you are and your contribution to this world.

So without any further ado, let's go on this journey into adulthood together. Let's grow into the remarkable human beings we were meant to be!

BUDGETING AND BANK ACCOUNTS

"You must gain control over your money, or the lack of it will forever control you."

— DAVE RAMSEY

*Y*ou may think little about the value of money and whether something is value for money. You may know how much a new pair of Levi's jeans or a new video game costs. But this differs from what I'm talking about when I mention value.

Think about when you head out to the store (shops) and see the shelves packed with many items. Each is the same thing, like canned (tinned) tuna, but there are over 10 brands, and the prices range drastically. To each of these brands, the value differs. The value comprises several factors, such as cost, quality, and sustainability. You may need help determining how much you should spend on a can of tuna because what you see initially is just the advertised price. You may need to determine if you are paying for quality or other factors. You may have a favorite brand you have tried before that you enjoy most, and it isn't the most expensive or the cheapest brand on the shelf. But, over time, you have learned that you get the most value for your money in this specific canned tuna brand.

Now, you may face multiple brands for items you need, and everything costs money. If you go shopping with the notion that the most expensive item must be worth more or better, you will run out of cash fast! **Tip:** It's worth trying the cheaper brands; you can research sustainability and quality online if that is important to you, so you feel more informed. You only need to do this once but will be able to buy more confidently next time. An example is brown sauce, the store-brand version of brown sauce may be just as good as the well-known brand. Stores often re-label quality products in their own name, so they are worth trying and saving money simultaneously.

BANK ACCOUNTS

When you start with money, one of your first considerations is where to put it so it is safe and can work for you. You will need your cash in a bank to operate in the modern economy.

Firstly, choosing a reputable place you trust with your money can seem daunting. Especially if you are moving your money from your piggy bank to a digital database where you never touch any physical cash.

In reality, some bank accounts and banks are better than others. Some accounts will have different fees and ways for you to access your funds. Some may be longer-term saving accounts that require official notice before withdrawing funds. While others may allow immediate access. The difference between the two may be that you can earn interest in the former option but no interest in the latter.

Additionally, depending on your age, your account may need to be linked to a parent or legal guardian. As we will see with loans and investment opportunities, you may need to shop around to find which accounts best suit your needs.

How do you figure out what you need the bank account to do? You can have an account into which all your allowance and birthday money can be transferred, and when you start working, you can keep the same account and account number. One significant difference is that before you are 18 years old, you are not legally allowed to have an overdraft. This is when you can withdraw more money than is available in your account. The money is essentially borrowed. Once you turn 18, you can apply for an overdraft, provided you meet the additional requirements other than age. The bank will likely charge you for using it. You want to avoid being in a position where you use your overdraft regularly. It will cost you more in the long run.

Note: Banks are profit-making businesses. They make money from you depending on the banking services and the type of account you choose. Keep this in the back of your mind. It's easy to forget and think banks are just big friendly piggy banks that hold your money for you. At the end of the day, they are in business to make a profit.

COMMON TYPES OF BANK ACCOUNTS

From the age of 11, your parents can establish a checking (current) account for you in which you can set up a banking app or an online banking profile. You can make direct transfers, receive direct transfers, pay for apps on Google, withdraw from an ATM, and so much more. If you are over 16, you can apply for this bank account yourself. Alternatively, your parents can set up a savings account for you where you will need more time to access the money. Still, depending on your chosen option, you will be privy to some great interest earnings that are not taxed.

If you have a holiday job or are over 16, you should have some say on your account type. But it is always best to speak to your parents or guardian and have their direct input in ensuring that you stay responsible with the finances you earn. It is best to choose an account that caters to your needs. You choose whether or not you would like to have a prepaid card loaded with your money. Where the money is depleted or more is added to the card. Or to have an account where the money is stored in the bank.

Aside from choosing an account that best suits you, think about the access you'd like to have to your funds. How often do you need access to your money? How will you withdraw money from your account? Will you be paying for things online? Can you log in online and manage your money that way? Do they have an app for your mobile? You can't do this for most children's accounts, so if this is what you currently have and want to manage your money online, think about upgrading to an adult account. Remember you also need to consider the account fees you may be liable to pay monthly. They differ from bank to bank and between different account types.

Most common bank account types you will come across:

- **Checking (current) accounts** - used by most adults for everyday use. Most banks will have various checking (current) accounts with different features and fees. **Tip:** Don't get an account with services you think might be nice but don't yet need. Or choose one with the flashy-looking debit card. Start with something basic. It will be cheaper. Upgrading to a more premium account is easy and can be done later once you are up and running and know what you need.
- **Student accounts** - a type of checking (current) account. The account may allow lower balances, understanding that students have less money. Some banking fees may be waived or lower than a standard adult account.
- **Children's bank accounts** (up to 18yo) - access may be too limited for your growing needs. If still under 18, compare against adult checking (current) accounts and time your move. **Note:** You don't need to stay with the same bank if

you already have a children's account. Another bank may suit your needs much better.

- **Savings accounts.** We will cover these later in Chapter 2.

Tip: There are many websites where you can compare bank accounts. Some sites to try: investopedia.com or moneycrashers.com for bank accounts in the US and money.co.uk or moneysupermarket.com for bank accounts in the UK. There are many other good sites. You can use your search engine to find them. Comparison sites may receive a commission for referring you. They may not be as independent and unbiased as they appear. So, once you have a good idea of the bank or banks you prefer - go directly to the bank's website and revalidate the information and ensure it all stacks up.

OPENING YOUR ACCOUNT

When you are ready to open your checking (current) account, there is some personal information that you will need to provide. In some cases, depending on your age, your parents may be required to provide similar documentation.

Living in the US, you will need the following:

- Your social security number.
- A valid government-issued ID (an identity card, passport, or driver's license)
- An opening deposit. Which may vary from bank to bank and account type to account type. Typically $25 or more.

Living in the UK, you will need the following:

- To fill out an application form, which can be done online or in a branch.
- You must provide your name, date of birth, and address.
- Two forms of ID. This can be your passport, driver's license, identity certificate, or birth certificate.
- An official letter or bill addressed to you. However, considering that you may not be at an age where you are receiving any bills or official letters, the bank may accept a letter from someone who can pass as a character witness, such as a doctor, teacher, or a social worker (Citizens Advice, n.d.).

MONITORING YOUR BANK STATEMENTS

Once you get your bank account and start accessing your money, you must check and monitor your bank statements. It is an easy step to forget or overlook.

Your bank statement is issued to you every month. Either digitally or printed - most banks message you that your bank statement is available online to view or download. Your bank statement details every transaction that has been made on your account. You need to look at your statements, often with a magnifying glass, and ensure that everything is in order. There are many reasons why you need to closely check your statement and a number of ways to do so (Popoola, 2017):

- Fraudulent transactions: You want to look at your statement to confirm that no unauthorized transactions have been made on your account. You may receive a text message notification when transactions are made. These amounts may sometimes be so small that you are not automatically notified. Small transactions that go ignored for an extended period can accumulate and lead to money lost without you even noticing. If a long time has lapsed, there may be nothing that your bank can do about it. However, they will show on your bank statement, meaning you can stop theft.

- Loan application: If you are applying for any large loan, such as a mortgage, a car loan, or even a credit card, the place from which you are taking the loan is going to want to ensure that you are financially viable and they are going to do so by comparing your expenses to your income. This will tell them whether you earn enough income to pay your monthly installments. It also shows whether or not your income is stable.

- Tax filing: Taxes are in a league of their own, and how you file your taxes may differ depending on your job or if someone is doing your taxes for you. If you are filing taxes for itemized deductions, you will need your bank statement as proof that these items have been paid from your account.

- Credit report: A bank statement will also be used for your credit report when verifying that your credit report is correct.

- Monthly budget: Your statement is essential to creating your monthly budget. Using it as a guide, you know exactly how much and what you spend. With the monthly bank statement, you can further optimize your budget by using more than one month's bank statement information. Checking the average amounts you spend. You will know your spending history and can track your budget at the end of every month.

Suppose you are looking at your bank statement for the first time. Seeing all these numbers, abbreviations, and reference numbers may be overwhelming. But there is a way to read a statement and know what you are looking at.

Many common factors in a statement are standard no matter where you live in the world. Before you reach the transaction details, you will see your personal information and the bank's information in the panel at the top of the first page. These details will include what period the statement is for, your account number, full name, and address. It will also have the bank's details, such as their head office address or your branch address, a customer care line, and an email address. Depending on the number of transactions you make in a specific period, usually a month, your bank statement can be one or multiple pages.

The transaction section will include details for each transaction that was made, including:

- The date
- The type of transaction (if it was an automated payment, direct debit, standing order, withdrawal of funds, direct deposit, or bank transfer). Your bank will use abbreviations. If you are still determining what each one means, you should be able to find a glossary on your statement or on the bank's website. Don't worry; you will become familiar with them all soon enough.
- The amount of money transferred.
- Whether it was a debit (paid out such as a bill) or credit (paid in such as a salary). It may even have the columns "Paid In" or "Paid Out" instead as banks try and become more customer-centric.
- Your running balance after every transaction

An opening balance will show your money in the account before all the transactions for that period are recorded. The closing balance is the amount left in your account after the statement period's transactions.

Your bank statement's opening and closing balance may not reflect what is in your account at the precise moment you receive your statement. This amount may differ if you check your banking app or online service. This is because your statement may be from the first of one month to the first of the next month, and you may only receive your statement on the third of the month. Transactions may have taken place between the date that the statement closed and the date that you received it, and these transactions will be recorded in next month's statement.

Tip: You can check your transactions at any time with online banking. You don't need to wait a month. You can check any date range. If, for example, you want to check something that is worrying you, log in and check it as soon as possible. Perhaps you were overcharged, charged twice, or received a notification that an unknown amount had been taken from your account. For peace of mind, jump on it as soon as possible. You are in control and responsible for your money. Once you feel in control, it's empowering and gives you a sense of well-being.

DIRECT DEBITS

A great way of making sure you remember to make and keep track of payments is through direct debits and standing orders or automatic withdrawals. Direct debits give businesses approval to take money from your account on an agreed-upon date, which will be verified by an agreement between you, the bank, and the business.

- To set up a direct debit, you complete a mandate-style form, either a paper copy or electronic format. The business wanting payment will provide this to you.

Tip: You can often get a small discount on a bill if you agree to pay by direct debit. But also, be aware that the amount of money businesses request each month can vary for direct debits.

A reason you might want to cancel a direct debit early is if a company takes vastly varying amounts each month based on estimates they calculate. Or you need their payments corrected each month. In these cases, you may need a more hands-on approach, firstly with getting accurate billing and secondly getting a payment method that works for you, not just them. An example could be an estimated utility bill for electricity. First, ensure you have the bill and check the meter reading usage they have estimated. If this is far from your actual usage, submit your accurate meter reading immediately. Then ask for a revised bill. It's best to provide precise meter readings regularly. This helps avoid these situations. You can do this on their website or over the phone. If you don't contact them, these issues don't go away; they escalate and compound, but most can be remedied quickly.

- To cancel a direct debit, a 2-step process is advised. Log in to your online bank account, and click on the direct debit section of your account. You will see all your direct debits, old and new. Click the one you want to cancel and cancel it. Then contact the business it relates to and advise them it has been canceled. This can be done by phone, or they may have an email address for customer support or billing. I have experienced a company taking the payment amount even though I canceled the direct debit - because I never contacted them. So it's best not to chance it.

If you still need to pay these bills regularly, remind yourself each period it is due. You may be able to opt for email or text message prompts. Check the bill is correct and make the payment. Watch out! Frequent late payments may get you a bad credit rating.

STANDING ORDERS OR AUTOMATIC WITHDRAWLS

In contrast, a standing order, or automatic withdrawal, is when you instruct the bank to pay a set amount to a recipient at a regular frequency, i.e., monthly. This is verified by an agreement between you and the bank, which is money issued by you. The only responsibility you will have is ensuring sufficient cash in your account for these transactions.

- To set up a standing order, log in to your bank account. Search for the standing order section (usually in the same place as direct debits), and add your new standing order there. You will need their bank account details, the unique account number, name, or reference number they recognize you by, and the agreed payment amount.
- To cancel a standing order, log in as before, search for the standing order section, choose the relevant standing order, and click cancel. The same as canceling a direct debit - if you still need to pay this amount regularly - set reminders each period it is due. Remember to cancel the standing order when you no longer need it.

USING AN ATM

While many believe that when machines rise up against humans, ATMs will be leading the rebellion, until then, Automated Teller Machines provide us with access to cash whenever we may need it. The world is becoming highly optimized because the need for physical cash has been reduced. After all, payment machines allow you to use your debit or credit card directly. However, there are still situations that call for the use of cash. Every checking (current) bank account you have will have a card linked to that account. This is the key to unlocking your access to money. Most banks also allow contactless payments using your mobile phone or Smartwatch.

If you want to withdraw money from an ATM, it's best to use an ATM machine linked to your bank, or you may incur a fee.

To withdraw cash:

- Insert your debit card into the machine.
- Enter your pin. Be sure to memorize your card-specific pin and know it by heart.
- Select the transaction type or service required.
- If asked, select the relevant account.
- Enter the amount you wish to withdraw.
- Once the transaction is processed, you will remove your card.
- Collect your cash from the machine.
- Remember to collect your receipt if requested.

Having the correct card and pin number to access your funds is vital.

To make a deposit at the ATM, you must ensure that the machine is compatible with the function. The process will also vary slightly depending on whether you are depositing money into your own or another account.

- Insert your card and enter your pin.
- Select the option to "deposit" money.
- Follow the prompts about how and where to insert your cash or cheque into the machine, but ensure that there are no staples, paper clips, or folded notes.
- Confirm the deposit and the amount, then remove your card.
- Remember to collect your receipt if requested.

Make yourself aware of any fees associated with using an ATM and certain transactions. When you know the associated fees, you can make a well-informed and wise choice about whether it may be more cost-effective to withdraw cash or to use your card.

TRANSFERRING MONEY

There are many ways and reasons to transfer money to someone else. Whether paying rent to your landlord or sending a monetary gift to your friend. You may be scratching your head about how to successfully transfer. Since most banks have digital interfaces that you can access through mobile applications. You can log in to your app and transfer funds if you have the recipient's banking and personal details.

You could deposit the money directly at the bank or an ATM (similar to the method mentioned above). Or you could transfer the funds through money transfer apps such as PayPal, Venmo, and many more. You can also make a wire transfer if the recipient banks with a different institute than you or if the recipient lives abroad. There may be a two-step process when setting up a new recipient to which you want to transfer funds. They may want you to verify yourself through your banking app, via a call, or send an electronic message to your mobile. To set up a new recipient, you will need their name on the account, account number, sort code, and possibly who they bank with, i.e., the bank's name.

You will need slightly different account information if the funds are going overseas. A Swift code (Society for Worldwide Interbank Financial Telecommunication) or

BIC (Bank Identifier Code) and the IBAN code (International Bank Account Number). The Swift or BIC works the same way as a sort code, and the IBAN is a more extended version of the account number. The codes are a mixture of letters and numbers. The person you are sending funds to should provide you with these codes. If someone from overseas is sending you money, you can find these codes on your bank statements.

Warning: Please **be alert** when sending and receiving money from people you don't know. There are many scams around. If you are ever uncertain about a banking transaction and have only communicated electronically, always double-check that you are sending money to the correct person. You probably know them, so **call them**, match the voice, and check that they have requested the transfer, not some cyber-criminal. Only transfer the money if you are still sure. If you feel pressured or something feels off, contact your bank directly and get their advice. They can put you through to a specialist team. It's worth mentioning it is equally suspicious to receive money from strangers. It could be a step in their criminal activity. If you receive money either; in your bank account or if you use an app or account for other payments and have received an amount that isn't yours. First, ask the person who sent it to cancel or reverse the payment. Do not send them the money if they say they can't cancel it. Do nothing with the amount. If the money is in your bank, contact your bank. If it is in another type of account, contact that company and ask to speak to someone - the same as you would the bank. In both instances, you may need to talk to their fraud team. They will take as much information from you as possible and investigate it further. The most important thing about this step is that they protect your money and ensure your account has not been compromised.

BUDGETING

Budgeting can seem scary to some and just deprioritized by others. While budgeting and money management can be overwhelming and sometimes difficult. It raises questions such as: What if I can't stick to my budget? What if I go over budget? How do I know if I have earmarked enough of my budget for this item I need to buy? These were the questions that plagued me, and I'm pretty sure this is what you have faced, too, at some point. The reality is that you will not get the hang of it on the first try. It takes work and effort. You may make errors once or twice, go back in, and readjust your budget, but finally, you will get there. And that is alright; it's part of the budgeting process.

WHAT IS A BUDGET?

Budgeting comes down to knowing what comes in and what goes out financially.

Ultimately, your aim is for your outgoing cash to be less than your incoming cash. But where do you begin? Whether you are starting a new job or are a student receiving a stipend or an allowance. You need to know how much money is coming in. Ideally, you would live within your means, funded by how much money you receive monthly or weekly. When you have more expenses than your income, it will be harder to survive. Understanding your income before deciding which place to rent is best. If you have an income that varies from month to month, the best way to plan your budget is to calculate it on the lowest amount you are expected to receive each month. That way, when you earn more in months, this can go into your savings as a surplus and be used to subsidize any shortfalls you may experience later.

HOW DO I CREATE A BUDGET?

When creating your budget, it is best to categorize it. The first category will be your income, next your savings, and the last category will be your spending. Which will further be divided into "necessary expenses" and "other expenses."

Your savings is where you will list all the savings goals you are hoping to achieve. This is the money you will set aside and that you will not be using. If you want to save for a new car or an apartment deposit, set this money aside. I recommend keeping some funds aside for the unexpected. This means you are putting away a stash of "emergency" cash just in case. This can help you if you ever find yourself in a situation where you need some financial assistance. Hopefully, these financial emergencies don't arise too often. Examples might be: unforeseen car troubles, if you need to fly somewhere for an interview, visit family, or for any other reason. **Tip:** Keeping a little extra in your bank account also reduces the risk of you going into your overdraft whether agreed with the bank or not. Usually, there are penalty fees in both circumstances - so keep that buffer amount in your account!

In terms of spending, you have necessary expenses, which you need to pay to survive. Things like rent money. Suppose you still live at home with your parents and are not expected to contribute to the utility bills. In that case, you may still need to budget for: car fuel, vehicle payments, phone bills, or groceries. Or anything else you couldn't possibly live without long-term. By the time you start planning a budget, you should have an idea of what your monthly payments are. You should know what needs to be paid and by what date. I mostly automate my payments and set a date for the day after payday. Then, I tick off my budget as each payment is made.

Other expenses are different things for which you pay. These can be gym memberships, your Netflix subscription, or the money you spend when you head out with your friends. If you do find yourself in a financial bind. These are the expenses you could and would look to reduce or eliminate from your spending; they are nice-to-haves.

Now that you have your categories listed and named, you can begin assigning a monetary value to them. This process will only start when you know the value of each item in each category. Here are some suggested categories for your budget plan:

- Income
- Expenses (necessary)
  - Rent
  - Groceries
  - Utilities
  - Car payments
  - Fuel for the car or transport costs
  - Clothing (the necessary kind)
- Other Expenses (nice to have)
  - Entertainment inc. Netflix
  - Going out with friends
- Savings (covered in Chapter 2)
  - Emergency fund and buffer
  - Deposit for a car
  - Savings (high-yield)

After you have defined your categories, you will then be able to choose a budgeting strategy. Consider the zero-based budgeting strategy. This means that after you receive your income, all money gets earmarked and allocated to a specific function, which includes savings until you hit zero, and you start again from scratch next month (Mint Life, 2021).

Alternatively, you could set aside your savings first or use the 50/30/20 rule whereby 50% of your income is designated for necessary expenses, 30% for other costs, and 20% for savings.

HOW TO MAKE BUDGETING EASIER

Take your time with the whole budgeting process. A great way to keep yourself motivated and encouraged to stick to your budget is to set financial goals for yourself. Are you hoping to go on a vacation with your friends? Are you saving for something important? Use this as the motivation to stick to your budget.

Another way to make budgeting easier is to track your spending every week or every month. No one wants to look at their bank statement at the end of the month and not know where their money went. Or constantly feel worried about paying for the basics.

I faced this when living alone, I didn't plan my meals, so I made dinner of sorts for one person every meal-time. I bought my meal ingredients from the local convenience store instead of bulk buying from the larger, cheaper stores (supermarkets). I could have cooked in bulk. I also went through a hotdog and instant mash-potato phase when I only had the coins left in my coin jar! Not a nice feeling at the end of the week. I decided something had to change and began planning my weekly meals and shopping. If you don't feel like eating the same thing two days in a row? That's alright, freeze the leftovers and reheat them another day.

The thing about budgeting is that your first efforts will not be your finest. You will get better over time with adjustments and practice. Remember that every aspect of life changes and develops. You may find yourself changing jobs, moving houses or apartments, or with two more additional expenses in a year than you currently have. In all cases, your budget will need to change and adapt. But on a more immediate point, I recommend giving yourself three months on your current budget plan and adjusting it if you are over-spending in certain areas. Especially if that over-spending is on necessary things. You will make financial mistakes—this is a reality, just part of the process—but the important thing is that you learn from them and always give yourself some breathing room. Perhaps you forgot it was your friend's birthday. Allow yourself some space to put a little less into your savings and buy your friend a gift.

Another way to make budgeting easier is to increase your income. Suppose you have the ability and the capacity to form a side hustle. I would 100% recommend that you pursue this avenue. If you enjoy baking on the weekend, sell your cupcakes. Take on some free-lance writing gigs if you are passionate about writing. But check your side hustle's profitability. The costs should not exceed the earnings! And remember to allow some money for taxes, so you aren't surprised with the expense later.

Lastly, try to be thrifty with your finances. Refrain from allowing your friends to influence a lifestyle you can't afford. They may have other forms of income to support a more lavish lifestyle, and I guarantee your time will come. But first, you need to start managing what you have and work your way up. If you need help managing your finances, feel free to ask for help from your bank or someone you trust. People dedicate their lives to managing finances, and these are the people that can help you.

It is essential to stay patient, especially if you find yourself all alone as a college student. If there is still time, set some money aside with your parents or a trusted family member before you head off to college. Start saving at least six months before you are set to go, or earlier if you can. Leave the emergency stash with your family so it is inaccessible to you. If you fall short, you can reach out to them and ask for some financial help without any guilt or shame because that money does, in fact, belong to you.

If your budget gives you an amount of spare cash you don't intend to save - it may be your socializing allowance. Consider withdrawing it from the ATM and paying for things the old-school way with physical cash. See where it is going. You can also physically check how much you have remaining. I'm not saying carry around a wad of notes, just a daily allowance. Example: If you are having a night out with friends, it's easy to overspend, so only take out what you have budgeted for. Knowing your bank balance is protected and accounted for will give you peace of mind. You will thank me in the morning!

Budgeting, tracking your spending closely, checking your bank statements, and using cash are ways to ensure your money doesn't disappear without your knowledge. But once you have a handle on your finances and you become better and better at budgeting, you are guaranteed success.

2

SAVINGS, INVESTMENTS, LOANS, AND HOW TO IMPROVE YOUR CREDIT RATING

"Don't let making a living prevent you from making a life."

— JOHN WOODEN

a basic understanding of interest rates is essential. Interest rates impact your savings, investments, and any loans you may need, and, therefore, the choices you have to make.

INTEREST RATES

A country's central bank sets the interest rates, displayed as a percentage (%). These rates go up and down depending on several economic factors. While we don't need to deep-dive into all the workings, understand that the rate set - can be an indicator of an economy's health. Let us see how you are affected by interest rates.

INTEREST ON SAVINGS

We receive interest on our savings as a reward for saving with that bank or savings provider. For example, when choosing a savings account, your primary focus, apart from how you will access your cash - is the interest rate. You don't just want your money to be safe; you want it to grow in size. You put money in the savings account, and interest is added periodically at a percentage rate the bank or savings provider has agreed to pay. Interest rates fluctuate, and banks offer fixed and variable rate options from which you need to choose.

A fixed interest rate - the bank freezes the rate for a specified period. You want to lock in a high rate for savings and a low rate for loans and mortgages.

A variable interest rate - will go up and down for a specified period. This is a valuable product if you expect rates to move in your favor.

The higher the interest rate (e.g., 5% being better than 2%), the more you receive in return. Example (in any currency, i.e., $ or £): If you save 1,000 with 5% interest paid annually, you will get 50 added interest. So your new balance will be 1,050 in total. Happy days! What could be better than interest on your savings? Compound Interest!

COMPOUND INTEREST ON SAVINGS

When interest is added to your savings account, the total balance increases after each interest calculation. In the example above, we went from 1,000 to 1,050 in one year. Suppose you don't add any extra money. In that case, year two's interest is added to the balance of 1,050, at 5%, adding an additional 52.50. Making your new balance 1,102.50, and so on.

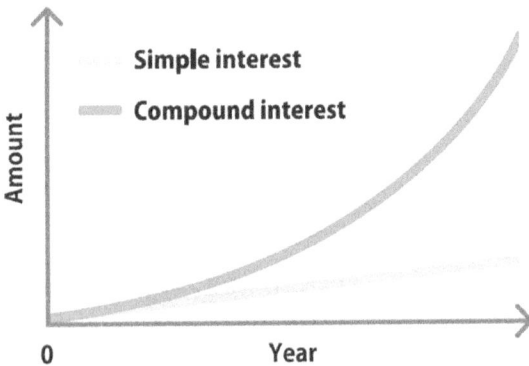

Term/Rate	Savings Interest Rate (compounded)		
	1%	2%	5%
Year 1	1,010.00	1,020.00	1,050.00
Year 2	1,020.10	1,040.40	1,102.50
Year 3	1,030.30	1,061.21	1,157.63
Year 4	1,040.60	1,082.43	1,215.51
Year 5	1,051.01	1,104.08	1,276.28

When comparing saving accounts, you will see letters after the percentage rate:

In the US: APY (Annual Percentage Yield) is used, i.e., 4.25% APY.

APY includes the inflation rate as an annualized rate and takes care of compounding interest. But before comparing savings accounts, you will also need to add allowances for any other bank charges or bonuses. As they are omitted in the APY figure.

In the UK: AER (Annual Equivalent Rate) is used, i.e., 4.25% AER.

Like APY, it includes inflation and takes care of compound interest. But AER also incorporates any bonuses or bank fees associated with that particular account, making AER quicker for comparisons.

Don't let the acronyms put you off! APY and AER are both helpful when deciding which saving options to choose.

INTEREST ON LOANS AND APR

If you have borrowed money in the form of a loan, you need a low-interest rate for the term of your loan (e.g., 2% is better than 10%). Otherwise, you could be at risk of paying back a substantial amount, consisting of the original amount you borrowed plus the interest.

Banks also give you options for fixed or variable interest rates on their loans, as with savings accounts. For loans, banks don't use APY (US) or AER (UK) but the APR (Annual Percentage rate). This rate includes inflation and includes the bank's service costs. All this is their fee for you to borrow and use their services.

Tip: If you need a loan, check that you're eligible first. Some require people to have a significantly favorable credit rating, which is difficult for young people to attain. There may also be other eligibility criteria. You can often do a preliminary check on the bank's website or discuss it with a broker. Once you know which loans are available to you, compare the APR rates, decide on fixed or variable, and check the small print. There may be other fees and conditions, such as a high administration fee to set up the loan or fees if you want to repay the loan early (early exit fees). Once you have all the information, make your choice.

Interest and Stocks (Investments)

In brief, when interest rates rise, it usually hurts stock performance. People want a better investment return when interest rates are on the rise. Stocks are higher-risk investment options than standard saving options. The demand for stocks decreases when interest rates rise. Also, when interest rates rise, customers and businesses reduce their spending, and this also causes stock prices to drop. Stock markets can also shift before any actual inflation increases or decreases. Suppose customers or businesses believe there will be an interest rate change soon. In that case, they alter their spending early, impacting the stock market.

Taxes

Income Tax

There is no getting away from this one. We must pay taxes on money earned when we reach certain pay thresholds. The thresholds are adjusted each year in line with inflation.

Social Security & National Insurance Contributions

In addition to income tax, you must pay Social Security and Medicare contributions in the US. Also known as the "FICA" tax. "FICA" stands for "Federal Insurance Contributions Act.".

In the UK, you pay National Insurance.

Seeing your first tax deductions on your paycheck (pay statement) is not much fun. You worked hard for your cash - how dare they take a chunk! So how do they use your money?

In the US, the big three categories of receiving your tax money are health programs such as Medicaid and Medicare, defense and security, social security, and repaying interest on government debt.

If you are employed (and have a boss) rather than self-employed (you are the boss), your employer will with-hold (deduct) all this tax from you. So you never physi-cally receive it, and they will issue a statement at the end of each year for you. You may hear these taxes called withholding taxes.

Interestingly, income tax can be split in the US into three pots: federal, state, and local (municipality) income tax. What you pay will depend on your state, as some states do not have state taxes.

In the UK, two-thirds of the taxes collected go to public services such as the National Health Service (NHS), schools, and prisons. A quarter is spent on state pensions and Universal Credit (benefits), approximately 5% on government investment, and approx 3% on repaying government debt. Like the US in the UK, your employer will withhold (deduct) this tax from you.

You are a small but significant cog in a big machine that supports the ever-moving and evolving economy. When you start paying taxes, you will find yourself paying more attention to the news and how the government spends your hard-earned money - and so you should! The global Covid pandemic has pushed countries to an all-time high debt, higher in most cases than in World War 2. Governments must expertly manage debt so nations can recover, and your taxes help do that when used correctly. Next election, listen to their policies and how much money they promise to spend on what. Food for thought!

Be aware other taxes relating to selling or renting goods, moving goods from state to state or country to country, property, gift, and inheritance exist. But you will be pleased to know we are not covering them here. That goes beyond the scope of what you need right now.

SAVING MONEY

How to Save

Placing the money you want to save into savings accounts will keep it separate from your day-to-day checking (current) account, which is a good idea.

Different savings accounts exist depending on the access you want to your funds and how much you have to invest. Ideally, you will want to invest in high-yield savings accounts at a young age.

Here are some savings account options:

- **Regular savings accounts**, usually have no bank card, are the most accessible but are not suitable for frequent withdrawals. The interest received is higher than a checking account. Remember, as mentioned above, to compare rates (APYs in the US and AERs in the UK). The rates offered may also be for a term, for example, 2 or 5 years. Each account offered will also state whether the rate is fixed (rate stays the same) or variable (the rate may go up or down). If interest rates are on the increase -

SAVINGS, INVESTMENTS, LOANS, AND HOW TO IMPRO… | 39

great news for savers; therefore, a variable rate may be preferable. Suppose the bank is offering a great fixed rate. You know the economy is improving; therefore, interest rates will likely fall. In that case, you may want to lock in that high fixed interest rate for a term rather than a variable rate that will fall too.

- **High-yield savings accounts** are similar to regular ones but should provide higher interest rates. They may be online only; therefore no physical branch to visit. These accounts usually have further limits on the withdrawal of funds. So you put your cash in and don't touch it for a prudent amount of time.
- **Other accounts** can include:

In the US,

- **Money market accounts** offer higher interest than regular savers. They also have some checking account features, such as writing checks, and may come with a debit card.
- **Certificates of Deposit (CD)** help you save a lump sum for a fixed period without direct access. If you withdraw from it, there are penalties. CDs are safer investments than

stocks, earning higher interest than regular savings and money market accounts.

In the UK,

- **ISAs** are perfect when you want to leave your money alone for an extended period, such as saving for your future as a deposit for a house. Importantly the compound interest is tax-free.

Tip: Check online when investing, as the government often provides incentive schemes. In 2023 if you are 18 or over and under 40 living in the UK, you can open a Lifetime ISA (LISA), and the government will contribute a 25% bonus to your savings. Up to a max of £1000 per year! Check out gov.uk/lifetime-isa

EMERGENCY FUND & CASH BUFFER

It can take a year to get an accurate view of all your expenses. If you have any annual bills, you must remember to add them to your budget. They are easy to miss, and you must have funds in your checking (current) account to cover them. We have all been caught out by unexpected expenses at some time or another. Suppose all your spare money is in a high-yielding savings account. An unexpected bill comes in, so you decide to withdraw enough to cover the bill. In that case, you will likely incur financial penalties for withdrawing the funds too early. That doesn't seem fair, but it happens often.

While Buffy (the Vampire Slayer) might keep the vampires from your door, a cash buffer can keep you out of the red and your overdraft. A cash buffer is a spare amount of money you should always keep in your checking (current) account. The value is up to you, but let's say it's ($/£)200. The benefit of this buffer is that it is significant enough to cover any small oversight. But not so big that you are missing out on substantial interest if it was in a savings account. The buffer alone is not enough to keep you out of trouble. Everyone should have an emergency fund. Life happens, and we need to be prepared for it because when we are, it lessens the blow and sets us apart as genuinely independent.

You can have more than one type of savings account. It is worth having a regular savings account and a high-yielding savings account. A regular savings account is easier to access. It is the perfect place for an emergency fund where you are less likely to incur any withdrawal fees and earn interest while it sits there. Then once that is set up, all your future spare money can go into your high-yield savings account to gain the best interest.

The trick here is to have a robust budget and plan for the unexpected.

Here is how you can do it:

First, get the buffer amount together in your account. To do that, you need to know how much. Look at your total budget for a year and calculate an average month's expenses (total amount for the year divided by 12). When you start out, it pays to have a higher buffer amount as you are more likely to underestimate your bills. One month's expenses is a prudent amount at the start. Also, round that number up to the nearest one hundred so you can easily remember the buffer amount when checking your balance. This buffer amount is your new baseline. Remember, if you have imminent bills due, you need more in your account than your buffer.

Keep most of your money in your checking (current) account till you have your budget up and running, so you can make informed decisions about what you need. You don't want to move your money too quickly into the wrong account types and incur penalties.

Second. Once the buffer is in place, consider where your emergency fund will come from. You want to put aside the equivalent of at least 3-6 months' expenses. Try to get this fund set up as soon as possible before you start saving. One source could be to reallocate any spare funds previously earmarked for saving. You could also try reducing some of the funds allocated for "other expenses," such as going out with friends. Transfer these emergency fund installments into a regular savings account. Do this each month until you reach your emergency fund target.

Third. Once you feel your money and the budget are broadly under control and with your buffer and emergency fund in place. You can move any money earmarked for savings to your new high-yield savings account.

So it happens you get an unexpected bill. You have your buffer and emergency fund, but you don't necessarily need them. Here are some of your options:

1. Contact the business or person from whom the bill is from and enquire if it can be settled in installments. They may say no or allow it to be paid over a period of time. Only do this if it is interest-free. You only want to pay back what you have to and only do this if they are known to be reputable. Utility companies are sometimes known to help customers smooth their bills out over a more extended period as part of being seen as customer-centric, putting

the customer's needs first. They would instead get their money back late rather than not at all in some circumstances. Regardless - it's worth the ask!

2. Adjust your "other expenses" activities and see if you can recoup the amount.

3. Increase your income. Can you pick up another shift, or do you have a side hustle that may help pay for the oversight?

4. Consider redirecting any money earmarked for savings, and allocate them to the bill instead.

5. You could use your buffer if it's for a small amount and if it is a one-off. As long as you can make an adjustment to fix the buffer balance the next payday.

6. Use your emergency fund. You may have also opted to set up an emergency fund with your family. If so, that, too, is an option.

7. If you are 18 or older, you may have an overdraft facility. You could use this, but you must use your buffer amount first to get near the overdraft. I mention this as an option, but there may be fees, and it can take a while to get back out of the overdraft and re-establish your buffer. Use your emergency fund before considering this option. Still, it's good that you understand this is an option, just not your best.

8. If you have a credit card, you could use this to pay the bill. Fees can be high on these cards. There is usually a 30-45 day grace period where no fees apply. This option is viable if you can pay this off before the fees kick in. In my experience, this rarely happens in practice. You will likely pay it off over a few months, even adding more expenses now your credit card is broken in. For this reason, this shouldn't be your first option. Unmanaged, it will become your most expensive.

9. If you need to access your high-yield savings account, that is still an option. It's not ideal, but life happens, so don't beat yourself up if this is the case.

10. If all else fails and you are struggling, ask for help. This could include the Federal Student's Financial Aid (US), Citizen's Advice (UK), or student support at your college or university. Otherwise, consider approaching your family or the bank in the form of a loan (which we will cover later in this chapter). Regardless of your circumstances, you always have options. As soon as you are aware you will struggle - seek help. You never know; there may be a grant, funding, discounts, or other aid or support you were unaware of.

If an unexpected bill or expense did come in, learn from it if you can. Why did it happen? Could you have done something to avoid it? Make adjustments as necessary. One of them would be to replenish your emergency fund and increase the balance to protect you from similar future unplanned expenses. Once successfully set up, nothing beats the feeling of being on the road to financial security.

If you are lucky enough to have a large sum to invest. In that case, it's advisable to talk to an independent financial advisor. You want the facts and details about all the options to make your informed decision.

GENERAL MONEY-SAVING TIPS

If you are reckless with your finances, consider tracking your spending. You don't need to carry a log book with you everywhere and make a note of every purchase. Still, there are apps available, including your banking app, which can help you monitor your spending. These apps can help you pinpoint where you are overindulging and can help you actively cut back.

You will also want to compare prices - remember the brown sauce from Chapter 1, and be aware of what you are willing to compromise on. Remember, cash has its uses; it's sometimes easier to manage and visible. You might be more unwilling to hand it over than just tapping your card or Smartwatch for payment.

INVESTMENTS

At your age, you may think that investment is just for older people or actual adults. My question is, "What makes you think you are not an adult yet?" And if you are still a teenager, my question is, "Did you know that you could invest as a teenager?" Yes, you could wait until adulthood to consider the prospects of investing. Still, the reality is that the sooner you start, you get the upper hand and have a longer term to watch your investments grow than if you start five or ten years later.

In basic terms, investing means putting your money into something that will yield financial growth. The guarantee of growth depends on your investment type. How successful these investments are based on past and forecasted growth.

Investments can include stocks, bonds, funds, investment trusts, real estate (property), commodities, cryptocurrency, and collectibles. When you're looking to invest, you will approach investment options with the same level of criticism as you would taking a loan. You want to ensure that the place or institution you invest your money with is legitimate because you do not want to be a victim of fraud.

From the age of 18, you can begin dabbling in a variety of financial investment opportunities. Younger than that, you will need the help of someone 18 or older.

A crucial piece of advice is to fully understand the type of investment you are considering. Do your research. You can seek advice from a financial advisor or any adult you trust. The important thing is to never let other people decide for you. No matter how much you may trust them. But instead, have them explain everything to you so that you can understand your options and make an educated and informed investment decision.

PENSIONS

Retirement seems like a long way away, but the sooner you start providing for your retirement, the better. Everyone wants to retire, and retiring at a reasonable age, between about 65 and 67, is usual, but some hope to retire early. Now, let's consider that you may live until age 85 (this could even be longer, and you could live to be 100). You should ensure you have enough money to care for yourself in your old age. Start saving for your retirement as soon as you can. Starting young and setting money aside where you can't tamper with it or access it is the best way to ensure you are adequately taken care of when the time comes.

Alongside our state pensions, we can make other provisions and investments. We won't need to access these long-term investments for a long time. Remember compound interest and how it works in savings. Well, this works for standard pensions too.

Here is an example (any currency can be used, i.e., $ or £): Suppose you invest 100 a month into a pension with an average 7% yearly return, compounded monthly over 40 years. Your school friend starts their pension 30 years later. They invest 1,000 a month for 10 years, also averaging 7% a year compounded monthly. After 10 years, your friend will have saved around 173,085. Your retirement account will be 262,481.

	Monthly deposit 100 per month		
Annual Rate of Return	4%	7%	12%
Term Year 40	118,196	262,481	1,176,477

	Monthly deposit 1000 per month		
Annual Rate of Return	4%	7%	12%
Term Year 10	147,249	173,084	230,038

Rates of return can go up and down. The average assumed rate of return for state pension plans in the

United States was 6.9% as of September 2022. (Anthony Randazzo, equipable.org, Oct 22)

While compound interest is a no-brainer, those retiring today see a different return on their pensions than their parents or grandparents. Some may have retired, seeing interest rates closer to 12%. There is also no guarantee that interest rates will be great when you retire.

Some pension plans may see no growth for several years but then have an excellent rate of return another year. Understanding your potential pension payout is key, as you may need to further provide for yourself in other ways. Many pensions let you invest in various funds within the pension itself. Some give you more choices than others. It may be prudent to choose a mixture of fund options or consider a portfolio of different retirement investments, not just a standard pension. Hedge the financial risk by not putting all your eggs in one basket! Some funds will perform better than others under different circumstances. It can pay to diversify. As soon as you start working and have a regular income, it will pay for you to speak with a financial advisor. You want all the facts about the past performance of funds, understand why they did well, and their forecasted growth. Is growth only possible if inflation increases? How risky is each option, i.e., how safe is your money? You don't want all high-risk investments! Ask lots of questions and do further research online. Again get all the information in front of you and look at all the options holistically. What will give you the best payout at your desired retirement age? You want them to educate you about all your options, then you decide what's best for you.

How Much Should I Save for Retirement?

There is no fixed number here, but as a rule of thumb, 15% of your salary is a good start once you are in full-time employment. Some higher earners save more. Don't rely on your state pension, and hope it will be enough. Make additional provisions for yourself when you can. Having a well-researched and managed retirement plan will give you the comfort that you will have financial security in your later years.

UNDERSTANDING INFLATION

It's good to understand the time value of money.

Take the pension example above, if you had been saving $/£100 a month for 40 years, giving you $/£262,481 saved for your retirement. The value of that amount would not be the same as it is today due to inflation. Let us talk about the cost of a pint of milk. Let's say, for example, 1 pint costs $/£1.00. Suppose inflation increases by 2% every year for 40 years. That pint of milk would cost $/£2.16 in the shops. Your money is not going to go as far as it does today. In fact, at that same rate of inflation, your $/£262,481 would only be worth $/£118,875 today! That's why it is also crucial that your retirement and savings policy's rates of return stay well ahead of inflation. Otherwise, you are losing value in your original principal investment.

Interestingly, you may see in the news about specific job sectors demanding pay increases along with other demands from time to time. Part of this is the link to inflation. If inflation has been 2% for several years, and if they have not received any pay increase or received less than 2% year on year, they are receiving less value as their pay needs to keep up with inflation. Remember, the price of a pint of milk is going up? Well, their salaries are not keeping up, so they can afford less when they go food shopping.

WHICH COMES FIRST, THE INFLATION RATE INCREASE OR THE INCREASE IN THE MILK PRICE?

It's a good question and could be either. The government calculates the total cost of regular items people buy— from milk to computers, holidays, and mortgage payments. This total price is called the Consumer Price Index. In the US, they also use other measures for comparison. Ultimately the governments decide what the inflation rate should be depending on what outcome they want it to drive. If, as a consumer, you have debt, you will want inflation to increase to drive salary increases which eventually help you make your debt payments. The original amount you borrowed is worth less over time due to the rise in inflation. If you are a pensioner, you will want low inflation as you won't want prices to increase further due to your fixed retirement income (low inflation keeps the milk cheap!).

BORROWING MONEY

Let us move on to borrowing. There are just as many loan options as investment and savings options.

UNDERSTANDING BORROWING

When it comes to finances, taking out a loan may have crossed your mind. Whether it was to pay your student debts or you are hoping to get a little extra money to pay off an unexpected expense. Whatever it is, there are many things you need to consider before you take a loan.

First, you must make sure you are taking a loan to pay for something that will yield long-term returns. That will equate in value to the loan you have taken, which will eventually be worth the repayments you make. For example, you will not take out a loan to pay for a meal at a fancy restaurant - because you have food at home.

Second, this will yield little significance toward your loan value. However, suppose you own some land and take out a loan to build a house. In that case, you will see a return on this loan either by renting the new place out or living in it yourself. Paying off that loan will yield more excellent prospects. Similarly, you might take a loan to support your studies and education. You will see a return on this loan through a higher-paying job, which will assist you in paying back your student loan.

Next, before you sign any formal documentation that binds you to a loan - ensure that the organization you are to borrow the money from is an authorized financial service provider. You need to be fully aware of the interest rate you will be paying and the exact amount of the installments you will make.

Pay off your debt with higher interest rates first. Pump any additional funds into these first to reduce the repayment term (length of the loan) and the amount you will repay. Which could be 150% more than the initial loan amount.

Growing up, you quickly realize that borrowing money is not the same as asking your parents for cash for a night out. Instead, borrowing money comes with a lot of strings attached. For example, it comes with paying back the borrowed money and the "penalty" in the form of interest.

There are endless borrowing options that you could pursue. Each has a different purpose and function, including student loans, credit cards, a mortgage, or any other type of loan. Always read the fine print and know what fees are associated with any loan you take. An essential aspect of taking a loan or borrowing money is the Annual Percentage Rate (APR). Simply put, it is not done for free when you borrow money. The APR is the cost you pay for borrowing the money (interest plus the fees of taking out the loan), expressed as a percentage. The lower the APR, the less you'd pay back over and above your loan amount (MyBnk, n.d.).

It is also important to note that when you repay your loan, try to avoid paying back the minimum amount. The more money you pay back on your installments, the faster you will pay the debt and the less interest you will pay by the end of your loan term.

Generally, there are about six types of loans:

- **Personal**: Within this variety, there are different tailored loan solutions that vary depending on your credit rating, the total amount of the loan, and the payment term of the loan (Automobile Association, n.d.).

- **Car**: These vary depending on whether you want to own the car one day, trade it in, or lease it.
- **Mortgage**: Money borrowed when you purchase a home. The parameters and variables considered when you take out a mortgage are vast. It will include factors like; your credit score, monthly salary, monthly expenses, the value of the property you purchase, and if you are paying a deposit.
- **Home equity**: A home equity loan, known as a second mortgage, usually has a fixed interest rate and a fixed payment period.
- **Credit card**: Another common type of loan is a credit card, where you pay back the borrowed money in monthly installments. Credit cards have great flexibility and excellent benefits if used wisely. Some, when used, can improve your credit rating. Be sure of these potential benefits before you sign up for a credit card. If used poorly, these cards can cost you more in fees than any benefit you would gain.
- **Payday loan**: This is the least appealing in that it is a short-term loan, and the entire loan amount is payable on the date the payment is

due. Because it is a short-term loan, the interest rates are incredibly high, and you find yourself paying back more than you may have expected. Avoid these if possible.

Choosing the one that is best for you can take time and effort. Still, if you compare the loan terms and conditions to what you need, it is generally relatively easy to find one that suits you.

There are many different types of loans and sources from which you can get them, including banks, finance companies, credit unions, and many more. In the same way, as you'd carefully choose what type of loan would best suit you, so would you choose the best financial institution to take a loan from.

STUDENT LOANS

While all these loan options sound fantastic, if you are a student, there may be only one type of loan on your mind now—student loans. We know that studying further means investing in yourself. Still, sometimes, the mere thought of the cost of investing in yourself through learning is overwhelming. Well, there are options for student loans that you could choose to suit your particular need, but student loans differ depending on the country you live.

In the US, students are often required to repay their student loans through a standard repayment within 10 years of being issued. As well as all interest accumulated. Additionally, you could also make repayments based on your income.

Suppose you find yourself hoping to avoid entering into student financial debt. In that case, there are other options that you could consider and qualify for, such as scholarships and grants. These are usually issued based on academic performance, so if you ever needed the motivation to put your best foot forward, this could be a significant motivating factor. If this is your scenario, Chapter 7 will be invaluable.

When you apply to study in the UK, you can get a student loan that is often paid directly from the borrower to the university (Lewis, 2018). No finances actually need to pass your hands. Also, the amount you see that is due specifically for "fees" is usually not the whole amount. As some student loans may also offer payment for living costs. But repayment of these loans in the UK depends almost entirely on your life after studying and the salary you earn after you enter the workforce. Once you start working, you are only expected to repay your student loan if you earn £27,295 or more annually. And you are only expected to pay 9% of these annual earnings. If you take out a postgraduate loan, you pay this back with 6% of your wages while also paying back your initial loan. After 30 years, all of your remaining debt is wiped. It is also wiped in the case of death. None of your beneficiaries will be liable to pay for your student debt. Interest for student loans has also been capped at 6.3%. Another essential factor is that you can apply for a student loan in the UK even if you are studying part-time. Repayments are usually deducted monthly through an automated payroll function (Lewis, 2018).

Good Debt and Bad Debt

When you hear the word "debt," you may not associate it with being good. We have been taught to avoid debt unless necessary. But debt is sometimes good. Bad debt refers to the debt that stops you from reaching your financial goals or success. It is usually the debt you spend so much time trying to pay back that prevents you from saving. Bad debt has a high-interest rate and usually leads you to spend money you don't technically have (Get Schooled, 2022).

Good debt, on the other hand, is debt that has low-interest rates and that helps you grow financially over time. One such example would be a student loan. This kind of debt allows you to invest in yourself. Those with a higher degree generally earn more than those without a university qualification. This debt is good because it enables you to reach your financial goals. Another form of good debt is a mortgage loan to invest in property. You could increase your financial gain by renting out this property. The debt you have taken from the bank gets you closer to achieving your financial goals faster (Get Schooled, 2022).

But don't let the title fool you—good debt can quickly become bad if you find yourself in a position where you cannot repay the loan. Or if you are unable to make the monthly installments for any reason. If you are hoping to invest in some good debt, there are some plans you can set in place to make sure your good debt doesn't go sour (McGurran, 2021).

1. Use your emergency saving fund. Suppose you have a credit card and have used it to pay several new bills. You could pay it off quickly using your emergency fund. You won't even need to use your credit card if you have money that has been saved.

2. Choose a spending plan that you will stick to for your monthly budget. This will include how much money you hope to save, expected monthly expenses, and miscellaneous spending.

3. Stick to your savings plan.

4. If you have a credit card, pay your monthly bill. Avoid paying the minimum amount. If you can, always

add a little extra to your repayments. This will shorten the payment term.

5. Only borrow the amount that you need from a financial institute. Don't try to take extra for the pair of jeans you really wanted, or else you are going to pay for that pair of jeans, with interest, for the next couple of months.

6. Keep your credit score strong by paying on time and paying extra into your loan amount.

OTHER WISE FINANCIAL DECISIONS

Another financial decision you will need to make, or instead not make, is to actively avoid getting into a **financial relationship** with someone. You should avoid cosigning with a friend or family member at all costs. Unless you are signing for a mortgage with your spouse. If, for any reason, the person you cosign with has bad credit or can't make the payments. You will be liable to pay on their behalf.

This next point may upset you, but bear with me and hear me out. Consider **canceling subscriptions** you no longer use or are responsible for paying even though other people benefit from your expense. If you have an Amazon Prime and a Netflix subscription, cancel the one you use less often. If you have friends or family members with profiles on your subscription, it's time to discuss splitting the cost. If they don't use their profile, they won't mind you canceling the subscription or removing their profile and changing the login details either.

CREDIT REPORTS AND CREDIT SCORES

Having a credit report is such a weird concept. After I have just told you not to get into too much debt and to have savings on hand, I am now going to tell you something that is almost the opposite. You see, to get a credit card, a mortgage, or a car loan, you need to prove that you are already good with credit and pay off your debt on time or faster. This shows that you are trustworthy and will repay a loan that someone else may give you. This proof is your credit score and is recorded on your credit report.

Often the only way to obtain credit from somewhere is to already have credit and be good at handling that credit. Your credit report will tell potential creditors, employers, and landlords how you have handled your existing or previous credit accounts. As an individual, you must make sure that this information is accurate and correct at all times. Suppose you hope to get a credit card or a loan for the first time. You may be subjected to higher interest rates as you have yet to prove your trustworthiness. Or you may be able to seek out creditors that lend to people who are applying for credit for the first time.

Once you have a credit history, you must maintain a good score. If you miss a few payments, that may lead to your score dropping. Regardless if you have a good credit record or are new to lending and borrowing, you should improve your credit score in preparation for later life.

While it can take a long time to improve your credit rating, some steps you can take will provide you with a faster and somewhat notable difference in your credit score.

If you are starting out, these steps will help get your score started:

- Opening and managing your bank account - showing you can manage your incomings and outgoings.
- Direct debits - set up one or two direct debits to show you can pay your bills on time. Only do this if you have enough funds in your account and bills to pay.
- Don't miss any payments - late or missed payments work against you, especially if they are escalated legally. Avoid this and pay on time.

- Electoral register - make sure you are registered at the correct address. The credit agencies use these to check you are who you say you are.
- Debt on your credit card - pay it off as soon as possible. Some credit cards are designed to help your credit rating but check the small print on these.
- Residency information (address and personal details) is accurate and correct, no matter where you live. On this same note, bouncing from house to house or apartment to apartment makes you seem like an unreliable borrower, which may drastically reduce your credit score. You want to ensure that your details are accurate for two reasons. First, you want to ensure potential creditors are correctly informed by accurate information. Second, you want to check for yourself if any fraudulent activity is occurring at your expense. You will also be able to fix any incorrect information, such as your place of employment if you have recently changed jobs.
- Subscriptions to Netflix and other streaming platforms can immediately improve your credit score, where you are responsible for the account.

Lastly, you are going to want to use your credit with discretion. Just because you have it available to you doesn't mean you need to make use of it.

Finance is an essential part of anyone's life. It is the tool you need to survive. Therefore, managing your finances and understanding the basics of your current and future financial health is essential. Although these first two chapters have only scratched the surface of everything, there is to know about finances. These are the building blocks you need to succeed.

3

FINDING THE RIGHT CAR, INSURANCE, AND DRIVING TIPS

"If you can't yet do great things, do small things in a great way."

— NAPOLEON HILL

*L*ife takes a natural and expected flow. Once you complete college, you get a job; the first significant debt you might get into is purchasing a car. Only a few people are in a position to get a car from their parents, and others are not even lucky enough to get hand-me-downs. The reality is that buying a vehicle is one of the first and most significant responsibilities that you will take on. This chapter will cover everything you need to know about calculating the necessary budget to buy and run a vehicle and what to look for when choosing and buying your first car.

BUYING A CAR

For the longest time, the type of car you drove was seen as a status symbol, and rightly so, since the car's value directly indicated what you could afford. But as time has shifted, the idealization the world has placed on cars and vehicles has shifted too. It is no longer how sporty or expensive your car is. People now pay attention to how economical their vehicle is or its environmental impact. All things considered, buying a car or any vehicle is not cheap. If you buy one cheaply, the running and maintenance costs still quickly build, and the risk is higher for second-hand cars. So buying a car is a big life decision. You need to know what you are getting into.

SET YOUR CAR BUDGET

Setting your budget is the first thing you must consider when buying a car. You need to know what you can and can't afford. You don't want to set your heart on a car out of your price range. The best way to begin budgeting for a vehicle is to check how much money you have left over after all your monthly expenses.

Once you have this estimated amount, set that money aside into a savings account for three months to ensure your budget and financial health can handle the additional expense. This amount you set aside can also be used as a deposit for your new car, depending on your chosen payment plan.

It is essential to know that buying a car doesn't just entail repaying the value of the vehicle. You also need to consider the insurance you will need to take out on your vehicle. The cost of your insurance depends on various factors. The first factor is your age. It has been statistically proven that those that are younger tend to experience more vehicle accidents (Moneyshake, 2020). This is because of their lack of driving experience. As you get older, the insurance rates do come down. But the age of your driver's permit (license) also influences premiums. This means that even if you are older, but your license is only two years old, you are not considered an experienced driver. So your premium may be higher.

Other factors considered when you take out vehicle insurance are; the value of the vehicle and whether it is a high risk, i.e., if it's a vehicle regularly targeted by thieves and if it's parked in a safe, secure, covered parking place.

For example, if you buy a car that is a strange or peculiar color, it may not be targeted by car thieves. Because it would be easily recognizable. However, cars that are generic in color are targeted more often.

They may also consider where in the country you live for localized crime levels.

Fuel Costs

The next car-related expense you will face is fuel, i.e., gas (petrol or diesel) or electricity (for electric cars). On average, gas (petrol and diesel) is much more expensive in the UK than in the US due to the extra taxes the UK government imposes on fuel duty. In the UK, the fuel cost can be as much each year as what is paid for a cheap used car. It's not uncommon to have a fuel bill of £5,000 per year. By comparison, US drivers see gas priced more than half that of the UK, with average costs per annum closer to $2,000 per year. The cost will differ depending on your car's fuel consumption, price per unit of fuel, distance traveled, and whether the vehicle is petrol, diesel, hybrid, or electric. For budgeting purposes, if you are doing some heavy mileage, ensure you have sufficient funds for weekly fuel payments.

To calculate the fuel cost for your budget, you can use this formula.

Fuel spend in a month =
(mileage/miles per gallon) x cost per gallon

This example is in UK pounds/pence, but use it just the same for dollars or any other currency.

Distance = 500 miles per month
Fuel price: 150.00 pence per liter
(to convert liters to gallons x 4.54609 = 1 gallon)
Therefore = 681.91 pence per gallon
Mpg (Miles per Gallon): 34.00 mpg

=(500/34.00) x 681.91
=10028.09p = £100.28 per month

The formula above can also be used for electric cars.

You need the cost for the electricity per kilowatt hour (kWh) and the mileage per kWh

Electric spend =
(mileage/miles per kWh) x cost per kWh

You can check your car's mpg online or calculate this yourself.

To calculate yourself:

Check your odometer for the miles traveled since the last refill. Then divide the miles traveled by how many gallons of fuel it took to refill the tank. This will give you your car's average mile per gallon for that period.

OTHER COSTS

You will also need to consider the **maintenance** of your vehicle. Cars need to be serviced regularly, as well as the **tax** and **CO2 emissions taxes** you would need to pay. Lastly, consider the costs and fees associated with your vehicle's **license** and **registration.** All these costs can be researched online.

In total, this becomes a reasonably hefty amount and doesn't include the costs of parking or the price of paying for the actual vehicle. It is also worth noting that while electric cars may be excluded from some taxes or are currently set at a reduced rate, this will not always be the case. Road infrastructures need maintenance and improvement, so governments will eventually change the taxing structures, so electric vehicles pay their way.

Your car budget may look something like this:

- Car deposit* (need upfront)
- Insurance (need upfront + renew annually)

- First instalment* (need upfront + monthly till paid)
- Sales Tax - US only (need upfront % differs per state)
- License & registration fee - US only (annual or every 2 yrs, sometimes can include insurance)
- Road taxes - UK only (need upfront + annually)
- Fuel (ongoing)
- Service and maintenance costs (ongoing)

*Costs may differ depending on how you pay for your vehicle.

Once you have made a list of all the costs of buying and running a car, you can search for one that meets your financial and transportation needs.

HOW TO CHOOSE A RELIABLE CAR

There are practical aspects to consider when picking a car. It may need to do more than get you from A to B. Depending on where you will be driving, you may be better off having 4-wheel drive for off-road terrain or if driving in extreme weather conditions. If you are to drive long distances, you will want a comfortable seating position and cup holders. How many seats will you need? You could offer a car-share service and take a couple other people to college or work, so don't get a 2-

seater. Will the trunk (boot) fit all you need for your job/hobbies? Will you need to tow a trailer? If so, towing capacity is an essential feature to look for. Does your vehicle need newer tech so you can listen to digital tracks? If you are tall, consider a car with a steering wheel with adjustable height. If you have a disability, you might have other considerations to make. Pull together your list of must-haves and those criteria that would be nice but optional. Within your budget, you are looking for the must-haves. It would be best if you were willing to compromise the rest for a good car.

Other things to consider or avoid:

- If you choose a **small car**, you often see better fuel efficiency, and servicing and insurance are typically cheaper. They are easier to park, and let's face it, they are quicker to wash! They are usually the most affordable upfront; savings and benefits will come later, too, in usage. This is the best option if you are on a tight budget for the next few years.
- Currently, petrol is cheaper than diesel, so compare **fuel prices** when ready to buy. Also, compare to electric cars, are there any free charge points at your college or place of work.

- Low-profile **tires** may look the business and have many benefits. Still, they can wear down quickly, are more expensive to replace, are uneconomical on fuel, and might get you in trouble on icy or snowy roads. You find these tires on some sports or high-performance cars. You can usually tell which they are by the large alloys.
- If you choose a car with low or lowered **suspension**, you are also more prone to scrapes. You need to be extra careful of the road and the speed you drive over ramps and humps to avoid damaging the lower bodywork, chassis, and potentially the exhaust. The drive quality is also usually reduced when you go over pot-holes and bumps.

WHERE TO BUY YOUR CAR

NEW CARS

If you buy a new car from a dealership, you will pay a premium for the vehicle. Still, you will be covered for at least three years if any mechanical or electrical faults occur. You want to consider a car with a high fuel economy, i.e., 50mpg (miles per gallon) is better than 30mpg, so you pay less for fuel. You also want reliability and good performance. You can do all this research online.

Also, check what taxes you will likely pay for that particular car and if the car increases your insurance premiums. Ensure the sum total is within your budget. The benefit of buying new is that there should be no hidden problems or expenses. You are not buying issues someone else may try to hide when selling their second-hand (previously-owned) car.

Tip: When buying a new car, you may get discounts on older plated models as the dealerships prepare to bring in new ones; this happens twice a year. But it will only be on the less popular models they struggled to sell.

To get the full benefit of owning a brand-new car, you want to keep it for at least five years, if not much longer. It has its most significant market-value drop in the first year and can lose approximately 40% in the first three years! You paid a premium for being its first owner. As the car comes out of its warranty period, you will be liable for maintenance costs.

Tip: If you are going to be on a strict budget but are lucky enough to have enough saved to buy a new car - don't! If you need a car, still get a used car. Your cash is best invested in your education and saved. There is plenty of time to get a new car (if that's what you want) once your career is underway and you have more stability.

USED CARS

DEALERSHIPS

Buying from a reputable dealership can give you peace of mind over what you are buying. Dealerships are likelier to have done vigorous checks and servicing, and they will be valeted (professionally cleaned). They may also sell it with a 12 months warranty. This can come with an inflated price tag but is the least risky option, so you shouldn't have any expensive surprises in the first year of ownership or even longer.

PRIVATE (BOUGHT FROM SOMEONE'S HOME)

This can be a cheaper option, and you may find a bargain, but you need to do your checks and be more thorough and vigilant. Once you have done your checks, you are also more likely to be able to barter on price. It may not have been professionally cleaned. Meeting the previous owner allows you to ask how it has been running. Are you buying from a lady who has kept it in a garage or a twenty-something that looks like a drag racer! Ask them why they want to sell and where they have been driving it. Use common sense and make your own judgments. If something doesn't stack up, it's best to walk away. They may just be trying to get rid of a car, causing them problems, and want to pass those on to you. Watch out; it may be over-valued, so do your homework on the car's make, model, and year and compare it to other cars at that price. Go with a price in your head of its worth based on the condition you expect. If you find issues with the vehicle above and beyond what they have already stated, start deducting that from the advertised value. It will cost you money to rectify issues. You will also have little protection if something goes wrong once you have bought it. So be thorough! When purchasing from a private seller, view the car at their home, not a public place, so you can check the ownership documents match the address.

Online

As with most things, you can also buy cars online. Consider everything you need to check before buying an unseen vehicle. You can purchase cars through eBay; for example. You don't want to click the "buy now" button without checking the vehicle first. You must contact the seller, ask questions, and visit and inspect the car. The seller may want a deposit via PayPal. Still, the seller and vehicle must be verified against the ownership documents before transferring any deposit. The best way is to do this in person.

BE CAREFUL: A friend recently tried buying a vehicle through eBay. They did a Facebook check on the seller after they spoke to them to verify their details and noticed they were local, and the facts checked out. The seller wanted a deposit before they went to see the vehicle. When my friend pushed on how to get to the address to inspect, they were vague and only gave a postcode. My friend arrived at the location, no one had heard of this person, and there was no vehicle for sale. Luckily my friend did not pay the deposit. The same day the seller deleted their Facebook account.

EBay has advice about what to be aware of when buying a car through them. I recommend you read their guidelines carefully. I can see how some people could get scammed.

If you are in the UK - eBay.co.uk:

Go to the main home page and follow the route below: (in some instances, you need to scroll down the page for the hyperlinks)

home > help & contact > buying > buying items > buying vehicles parts and accessories > safe buying tips

If you are in the US - eBay.com:

> home > help & contact > buying >
> buying items > buying vehicles parts
> and accessories > eBay motors
> security center

Genuine sellers will not entertain time wasters, so only enquire about and view cars you are serious about buying. If it's not what you expected, you can walk away.

After purchase, if you don't live nearby to pick up the car, transport companies can deliver the vehicle for you. You need to factor in this cost and research it beforehand.

Auction

Buying a car from an auction does come with significant risk. There is little warranty. Suppose you are after a popular vehicle. In that case, the competition will usually drive the price up to more than it's worth.

The reverse is said for other cars, and you may catch a bargain. It takes more work to thoroughly check the car beforehand. Private sellers often try to sell their difficult-

selling vehicles through auctions - cars that may be thirsty for fuel and expensive to run. Don't get emotional about a car. You may think you are getting a vehicle for a bargain and forget to check the fuel economy and regret it each week when you come to fill it up. Just remember to research, check the car before the auction as best you can, and stick to your budget. Also, there may be auction fees on top. Find out what they are first and make allowances.

WHAT TO LOOK FOR WHEN VIEWING YOUR CAR

When you view your car, follow a checklist to remind yourself what to look for. You can find some lists online, but they can look like this.

- Check the tires: Check the tread. If the tire treads are 3mm (4/32 inches) or less, you will have to consider replacing the tires soon and factor that into the cost.
- Exhaust Smoke: If there is black, blue, or white smoke escaping from the exhaust in plumes, there is a problem that likely will take money to fix. A little on starting the engine is normal, but more than that could indicate issues.
- Check the electrics: Try using everything electric, from the windows, wipers, air conditioning, seat adjusters, lights, radio, and

indicators. Anything that is not working, then the asking price needs addressing.

- Check the Bodywork: Here you are looking for repainting or replacement, which might indicate it has been in a crash. Check in the daylight for dents and scratches.

- Check the gearbox and clutch: This is more of a test of how it feels rather than how it looks. The car should go through the gears smoothly and without noise. There should be no loud noises, grinding, or resistance. In a manual (stick-shift), the biting point must be mid-way when lifting your foot, not when your foot is on the ground. If it is, then it needs either adjusting or replacing.

- Check for gaps in the panels: Check that the gaps between panels match, including color. A mismatch or significant gaps can indicate poor repair work after a crash.

- Windowscreens & Glass: In daylight, check the windowscreen for chips. These can turn into cracks, and if they are on the driver's view side (the car will fail its MOT in the UK), the chip needs to be fixed professionally or the window screen replaced. Check the lights for any fogging, cracks, and chips.

- Check upholstery: Check the interior for rips, tears, stains, and smells. Some smells are hard to get rid of, such as tobacco smoke.
- Check all fluid levels: Check the oil, coolant, etc. Low levels or leaks can indicate poor maintenance.
- Check for wheel accessories: Check that the spare wheel is in place and in good condition. The adapter for the locking wheel nut (lug nuts or alloy wheel nuts) and jack are all there. **Tip**: Keep the adapter for the locking wheel nut safe. It is unique to your car and helps prevent wheel theft!
- Check the oil cap: When you remove the oil cap, if you see a mayonnaise-type substance on the underside of the cap, this could be due to the coolant mixing with the oil. It could be a sign of head gasket failure.
- Wear and tear: Look under the car, check the exhaust condition, and look for rust. If the inside of the vehicle doesn't match the mileage, i.e., if the mileage is low but the wear and tear on the seating and steering wheel are worn, then ask questions as this doesn't correlate.
- Look for leaks: Leaks are easy to spot. Well-maintained cars won't leak. Many fluids are used under the vehicle (sometimes up to six),

and rust, salt, and age can wear these down.

Also, check under the bonnet (hood).

If you can take someone with you who is well-versed with cars or an actual mechanic, get them to make their own checks. This will reduce the risk of you missing something. Not everything can be checked, not without a thorough garage inspection. Still, you can minimize the risk, pay the right amount for the car, or decide to walk away.

Information You Should Ask to See From The Seller

In the US - before you buy:

- You need the "title of the car," which can be either a paper or electronic document with the 17-digit VIN number. This document will have the car's color, year, make and model, owner's name and address, and the date it was issued. Check the details against the vehicle you are buying. Once bought, you will need this document and proof of purchase to transfer ownership to you. You will need them if you ever want to sell, your car is stolen or impounded, or your vehicle was used in a crime before you owned it.

- An Odometer Disclosure Statement will be included with the title. This shows that the mileage captured is accurate.
- A Damage Disclosure Statement will be completed if the car has been damaged in the past.
- You can use sites to do your own checks; National Insurance Crime Bureau's free VINCheck site or, for a fee, CarFax or AutoCheck.

In the US, after you buy:

All the above plus +

- Once you are ready to buy the car, you complete a bill of sale (purchase or sale agreement), and both the seller and buyer complete this document and sign it. Photocopy these documents, as you will need to send the originals to the DMV.

In the UK - before you buy:

- The logbook (the V5C) - Used car history check. If in the UK, you need to see the V5C and double check the vehicle registration number (VIN) matches that on the V5C document. It will prove who the current registered owner is and is essential if any disputes are down the line. Also, if the VIN numbers on the log don't match the car's, ask questions. Ensure it's an original document with a watermark, not a copy.

- The sellers details. If a private sale, the seller's details need to match those on the V5C; otherwise, start asking questions (hence if a private sale, buy from their home address).
- Check the Service History. Ask for the service history (if a used car), details of any work carried out, and the vehicle handbook. The service history should have the mileage recorded and the date and name of the garage. It may also be stamped unless it's a digital record. The mileage captured in the book is also a good check against the actual car mileage at the time of sale. There are also online checks you can make. hpicheck.com Autotrader in the UK has a car checking service where you enter the registration.
- Other Checks. It is worth checking that there is no outstanding debt on the car. You want to ensure it will not be repossessed by a previous owner's lender. You can check this online for a fee at hpicheck.com. This site also does several

other applicable background checks, including; servicing, mileage, previous owners, write-offs, stolen car checks, log book checks, and more.

- MOT (Ministry of Transport). If the car is 3 years or older, the vehicle must have a mandatory MOT test. Ask the seller for the most recent MOT certificate. It will include any work that was or is still required on the car - ask questions. You can also check the MOT status online. Just search gov.uk/check-mot-status

In the UK, after you buy:

All the above plus +

- Get Proof of Purchase. Once you have purchased the vehicle, you should always get a receipt to prove you have bought the car. The registration number (plate number), mileage, and seller and buyer details should be included. The vehicle make and model and the amount purchased. You and the seller get a copy, signed by both parties and kept.

TEST DRIVING THE CAR

This is where you really get to test the car's performance. Take your time. You can do many checks, not just the check in the mirror, which confirms how great you look sitting in the driver's seat (RAC, 2020).

- How did it start? It may need a new battery or alternator if it doesn't start.
- Temperature gauge. Does the car start up from cold and warm? Did the seller warm the car first? If they did, consider why. You may need a new thermostat if the gauge rises halfway quite quickly and remains there.
- Clutch. To test the clutch, try accelerating up a hill in a higher gear at low revs to see if it slips. Also, try a fast start. Is there any juddering?
- Gears. Do the gears change smoothly? Are there any loud noises?
- Steering. Are there any noises? Does the wheel turn smoothly? Does it pull to the side if you let go of the wheel?
- Suspension. When driving over bumps, listen for clunky sounds.
- Engine sounds. Does the engine sound noisy, or is it running smoothly?

- Performance. How quickly does it accelerate? Is it as you expected?
- Brakes. Test them. Is it a clean stop? Does it pull to one side? Also, see if you can test the handbrake - on a hill is best.
- Driving position. Is your car for a short or long journey? Does this car suit your needs? Do you like it? Seemingly little things make a big difference.

I wanted two cup holders. One for me and my partner. We had a car that only had one - it was a pain and annoyed me every trip! Ensure you are happy before you invest.

GET A GOOD DEAL ON YOUR CAR

Do your research first. Check other similar cars in similar condition and the market price to know if you are getting a good deal.

Be polite & fair when you walk around the car and point out any issues. Just in case these have not been taken into account in the price. It also gives them a chance to see it from your perspective.

Most garages will negotiate on price. If something is wrong with the car, the discount you seek could cover the cost of rectifying it. Don't expect massive deals on second-hand vehicles. You may annoy them. Have your budget with you. Make an offer for what you think the car is worth based on its condition. This needs to be a price you can afford. If they go higher, you must be prepared to walk away. Don't be emotional. You will find something better.

The dealer may throw in extras rather than lowering the price.

Don't feel pressured to buy. You can walk away at any time. It doesn't matter if you have been there all day. Make the right decision for you.

Documents needed before you can drive away new and used cars

- Driver's license/permit.
- Insurance (can be a short-term cover to get the car home).
- Proof of payment or financing documents. If getting financing from the dealership, you will need the details below and possibly your credit score information.
- Bring a recent utility bill, bank statement, current debit or credit card, and a valid passport if your driver's license doesn't have your current address.

- Road tax (UK) if the dealership did not get tax on it. Note: the previous owner may have some tax already on the car.

PURCHASING OPTIONS

Once you have found your ideal car and signed your final forms (which may differ depending on whether you are paying cash for your vehicle or taking a bank loan). You will drive off the lot with the new expense you are probably excited about. And then, it is time for your first payment. This may be done through a direct debit, which we discussed in chapter one.

There are many ways that you can pay for your vehicle yourself if your parents are not in a position to purchase a car for you. If you are in a financial position to buy your own car, the best option would be to save up and pay for your car completely with your accumulated savings. This is obviously an ideal situation, but only a few people have the opportunity to save up enough to cover the entire cost of a car. Also, if this was the option you were hoping to take when buying your car, you would still be subject to the above-mentioned running costs to have a car.

The next and most common option is taking a loan to purchase your vehicle. In such instances, your relationship for repayments would be with the financial institution from which you took the loan and not with the vehicle's seller per se.

Lastly, you could lease a car on a long-term basis. When you lease a car, you will never own it, but you pay to use and drive it. It can be a more cost-effective option, but you are limited to the miles you can drive in a month or an agreed-upon time frame. Exceeding the limited mileage may incur higher costs.

CAR INSURANCE AND ACCIDENTS

In the UK, you are legally obliged to have car insurance as a driver. If you don't own the vehicle you are driving, you will need to be listed as a driver on the owner's insurance, even if it is for a short period. If buying your first car, you get your insurance after you have purchased it but before you drive it on the road, as the insurance broker will want the car's details.

There are three types of motor insurance in the UK (Association of British Insurers, n.d.):

- Third-party insurance: This is the most basic cover accepted by UK law. It covers you for the damage and injuries that may be caused to others if an accident has occurred.

- Third-party fire and theft: This also protects your vehicle against damage not caused in an accident and includes coverage for theft and fire.
- Comprehensive: This type of insurance covers everything. It includes the coverage provided by the above options, medical expenses incurred in an accident, and the theft or damage of a car's contents.

In the US, there are also a variety of insurance coverage options that you can choose from. You need your insurance before you purchase the car. A dealership will ask for proof of insurance before you can take your vehicle.

- Collision insurance is the most common and notable. This will only cover your vehicle in the case of vehicle accidents.
- Liability coverage (sometimes called Casualty insurance) will cover any damage where you are at fault.
- Comprehensive insurance (sometimes called other-than-collison coverage) will cover everything from injury during an accident, theft of your car and its contents, third-party claims, and everything in between - except collision incidents. There are less common options that

may cover different aspects, such as if your vehicle serves as your "office" and you work almost entirely out of it.

The best way to choose your insurance plan is to get quotes and compare options before deciding on the one that suits your needs.

Reducing Your Premiums

It can be overwhelming to hear the amount you are expected to pay for your insurance coverage. It is for that reason that there are some options available for you to reduce your insurance premiums (MoneySuper-Market, n.d.):

- Drive less: The less mileage you add to your vehicle, the greater the chance of keeping your premiums down because you're less likely to be in an accident.
- Pay annually: Instead of paying monthly installments, it is more cost-effective if you pay annually.
- Buy smaller and cheaper: Smaller and cheaper cars cost less to insure and are, therefore, necessary to reduce your payments.
- Be safe: Keep your car parked in safe and secure areas to reduce its exposure to heat, theft, and

damage.

- Identify your excess: Pay a higher excess to your insurance, ultimately reducing your monthly insurance costs.
- Use telematics. Telematics is monitoring software that can be installed in your car. Your premiums may be reduced if you are identified as a good and safe driver.
- Add a driver: Adding an experienced driver to your vehicle insurance may reduce the premiums you pay each month.
- Complete an advanced driving course. If you complete one of these courses, you are likely to have enhanced your driving skills and be less likely to have an accident. This can help reduce your monthly insurance costs.
- Stick with your parents: Being on your parent's car insurance for a bit longer may get you a discounted price.
- Avoid unnecessary claims, as you may receive a no-claims reward. You will prove that you are a low-risk driver, and it will lower your premiums.

Knowing that you can shop around for the best insurance is essential. You can spend time comparing quotes, and during the comparison stage, you will be sure to find one that suits you. There are comparison websites and service offerings dedicated to sourcing and comparing a wide array of quotes. However, not all insurance companies are included when using these comparison sites. It may be best to expand your search beyond these sites. Try searching for the top ten insurance companies using an independent site. You can also ask your parents or guardian who they use and recommend. Still, compare your research and findings against that insurance provider.

REGISTERING YOUR VEHICLE

In the **UK**, you will register your vehicle as soon as it is ready to hit the road. Registering a car is done by filling in the required documentation and submitting it to the Driver and Vehicle Licensing Agency (DVLA). But before you even purchase the vehicle, you need to make sure that certain aspects of the vehicle are in place. You must check the car's registration number, make, model, logbook, and registration certificate.

Once you buy your vehicle, it will be registered in your name. You will need to obtain a Ministry of Transport (MOT) certificate every three years. Once you have taken ownership of your vehicle and have the insurance all set and ready to go, you will need to pay tax for your vehicle before it is usable on any roadway (Gov.UK, n.d.).

Paying tax on your vehicle is first done when you purchase it, and it will cover the first year of driving. Thereafter, at a different rate, you will pay tax on your vehicle every 6 or 12 months (Gov.UK, n.d.).

The amount of tax you pay will vary depending on the type of vehicle you have and your CO_2 emissions. It will also depend on the listing price of the vehicle (Gov-.UK, n.d.).

In the **US**, a similar requirement is set to register your vehicle before you drive it. Your car would need to be registered at the Department of Motor Vehicles (DMV). You would need to meet the state-specific requirements for registering a vehicle, such as the documentation and the paperwork that is needed (RelocateUSA, 2016).

When you purchase a vehicle in the US, the value excludes tax, so you would need to pay the sales tax when registering the vehicle. If you are purchasing your car from a vehicle sales dealership, the registration will be completed there, and it will save you a trip and the long queues at the DMV. The dealership will also collect your license plate and registration fees, as well as your sales tax payments (RelocateUSA, 2016).

If you are buying your vehicle through a private sale, you must head to your local tax office to pay the property tax and then to the DMV to register your vehicle.

You will need to provide the title for the vehicle, a bill of sale, the selling price, the vehicle identification number (VIN), proof of your extremely important car insurance, and a valid US driver's license (RelocateUSA, 2016).

CAR TAX

Something that you should definitely remember to pay is your car tax. I know the word "tax" can make you want to shrivel up on the inside, but being a citizen of this world means it needs to be done. So what are car taxes, and why are they important?

Across the globe, a fuel levy or fuel tax is charged on purchasing diesel, petrol, and gas. This charge is added to the price per liter or gallon and automatically added to the final amount you pay when you fill the gas (fuel) in your car.

As the world attempts to move toward greener economies, taxes are also added to your vehicle for CO_2 emissions. Although not commonly seen in the US, these CO_2 emission taxes are frequently charged in Europe and the UK to make people more aware and conscious of using their vehicles. They hope this will encourage people to carpool or use other methods to reduce their CO_2 emissions.

On this same note, to encourage road users to move toward reduced CO_2 emissions, a significant incentive has been attached to electric vehicles, which are tax-advantaged.

Additionally, taxes are added to maintain and enhance the road infrastructure. This is why you may be liable to pay for road tolls, contributing to the upkeep of the most commonly used roads.

In addition to federal and state fuel tax, drivers in the US pay annual property taxes in most states. This is in contrast to the UK, where you must pay different taxes throughout the year instead of a once-off, once-a-year fee.

DOCUMENTS TO CARRY

Nothing is more nerve-wracking than seeing those blue and red flashing lights. Knowing that you are being pulled over by a traffic cop (traffic police), whether you have committed a road violation or not. You may feel fear even though you know you didn't do anything wrong.

But to reduce your stress and ensure you can breathe easily if ever pulled over in a routine stop. You need specific documents verifying your driving ability and confirming that you're allowed to drive that vehicle.

Whether it is yours and registered to your name or if it's someone else's and you have permission to drive the car.

The general documentation you would require every time you enter your vehicle is your:

- Driver's license
- Proof of vehicle registration
- Vehicle insurance

These are deemed necessary in the US or highly advised in the UK. Other documents that you are advised to carry with you are your:

- Vehicle manual
- A pen and paper
- Your MOT certificate (UK only)

In the UK, if asked and are found not to have the required documents, you may be asked to bring them to your nearest police station within seven days. In the US, you may receive a citation or a fine.

WHAT TO DO IN AN ACCIDENT

Accidents do happen. It is one of the things that make us intrinsically human. But how we respond to these accidents and mistakes defines our character. If you are driving in a parking lot (car park) or anywhere else and you bump into a parked car, there are specific procedures to follow. To ensure that you don't commit a crime by committing a hit-and-run and to ensure you don't become suspicious under the eyes of your insurance. Following these steps will also be a testament to your integrity.

Whether or not the accident was seen, and whether or not it was a big accident, handle every unfortunate situation with the same magnitude. If you do bump into a parked car, you should always stop. Never drive away, as committing a hit-and-run is a crime. Even if it was a minimal accident, you must turn on your hazards and assess the damage. There may be witnesses and cameras that see the accident. If you have been identified as the culprit in such instances, you will face more discipline if you flee than if you do the right thing.

Next, you will want to leave all your details, name, number, registration insurance details, and a brief explanation of the accident, be careful what you write. Insurance companies can use your comments against you when settling the claim. If you are not the owner of the car you are driving, you will need to leave the owner's contact details, and you will need to contact the owner and explain the mishap to them.

If in the UK, you are best to report the incident, not just to your insurance company but to the police. Some insurance companies ask for the police reference number. You can head to your nearest police station or call the non-emergency helpline (101 in the UK) to report the accident. When you report the accident, it is a good idea to have taken notes and have a detailed list and images of the damage and exactly what occurred (take photos of your car and the other car's damage).

In the US, it is usually the owner of the parked car that would contact the police (non-emergency helpline 311) as it is a requirement by many states to report vehicle accidents.

Look for witnesses and take their details. Police and insurers may want to ask them questions and check local surveillance cameras. Don't just drive off without trying to find or contact the car's owner. There is a good chance a camera has caught you in action, and if caught, you face points on your license, fines, and jail time if in the US.

Lastly, even if you aren't intending to make a claim for this accident, it is always a good idea to notify your insurance company of this occurrence. And remember, doors get dinged, and accidents happen. As long as you react appropriately, you are just as human as everyone else.

DRIVING TIPS

The day you get your license is the day you think you know everything there is to know about driving. But even the best and most advanced drivers go for refresher courses on vehicle handling and safety in different driving conditions. Consider what you learned and where you drove for your driver's test. You are only taught to pass your driver's test. You only experience some weather conditions and some road types during your test. This means that you, like everyone else, could use the extra driving tips, especially for safety purposes.

Previously, we discussed that those who are younger will find themselves paying higher insurance premiums because they are less experienced. This lack of experience means that younger drivers may need some extra tips. Some essential information that you should actively stick to (Cheshire Fire, 2019):

- Always drive the speed limit. It is no lie that
  speeding kills. When you drive fast, you have a
  lower reaction time and less control of your
  vehicle, and you may not see things as clearly.
  Speed limits set in towns and particularly
  around schools are vital not just for stopping
  distances but imagine if a child or adult steps

out in front of your car, and you hit them driving 20mpg (32kph); there is a 2.5% fatality chance. If driving 30mph (48kph), that percentage increases to 8% fatality risk. That percentage increases exponentially the faster you are going. (ROSPA, 2017).

- Always wear your seatbelt. After all, you're technically on a roller coaster that you are in control of.

- Make sure your car's headrest is in line with your head. Suppose the headrest isn't in line with your head and instead with your neck, and you have an accident. In that case, you will experience whiplash that will be made worse by the possible impact of the headrest on your neck.

- Keep your windscreen—and the whole car— clean. If your windscreen isn't clean and the sun reflects on it at an awkward angle, it could significantly impair your vision.

- Hold your steering wheel at a 9 and 3 o'clock angle. This will allow you to control the steering wheel more; should the airbag eject, your arms won't flail. This also gives you stability if you hit a pot-hole, skid on something slippery, or if your tire blows.

- Look left and right as many times as you need. This doesn't just apply when crossing the road on foot. Ensure the road is clear in both directions before proceeding to an intersection. The traffic light may tell you it's your turn to go, but another driver may not have control of their vehicle or may be driving too fast to stop. Regardless of signals and roadsigns, you must decide whether it is safe to go.

- Stay in your lane—figuratively and literally. Only change lanes and overtake when it is clear to do so.

- Never assume that a driver will stop in time or make other assumptions about someone else's driving. It is always better to be overly cautious than reckless.

- Take note of the behavior of others. Look out for aggressive drivers on the road.

- Be alert. Check for animals crossing, or if you are approaching a traffic light, be extra cautious and aware of pedestrians.

- Consider your lane positioning. If you are off to one side, you may give drivers around you an indication that you are turning off soon or want them to overtake. Drive confidently and assertively, and don't give the wrong signals.

If you have the opportunity, look for advanced driving courses or one-day courses that you can take. This will not only give you the skills you need, but it may also bring down your insurance payments.

DRIVING IN DIFFERENT WEATHER CONDITIONS

Driving is a task that requires extreme concentration and focus. Throw in some bad weather, and it has the makings to be a potentially catastrophic situation. But it is not always feasible to avoid going places just because of the weather. You may still have a class or a job to get to. When the weather is compromised, be extra cautious on the road.

HEAVY RAINS AND FLOODS

Remember that the rain makes the roads slippery, so you may have to drive slower than the speed limit. If you had to immediately hit the brake, the rain might reduce your tires' traction on the road.

These are some tips that you should keep in mind when driving in the rain (Cheshire Fire, n.d.):

- Keep your headlights on, whether it is day or night.
- Ensure your windshield wipers are working because it is crucial to see and be seen.
- Leave more distance between you and the vehicle in front of you than you usually would if you weren't driving in the rain.
- Don't try to drive through moving water. You may not be able to judge the speed and force of the water, and your car could be swept away.
- Try to safely avoid or slow down if you see standing puddles of water, especially if pedestrians are walking on the sidewalk.
- If you hit a standing puddle of water at a great speed, it can cause damage to your vehicle.
- Drop down in gears when going through a puddle of water because the high rev of the car will push the water out of the exhaust.

HIGH WINDS

When driving in high winds, there are some things that you need to be cautious of. Not only will you feel your vehicle pulling to one side because of the wind, but you also need to keep a close eye on any flying objects that may be blown into the road. If you have a relatively high vehicle, you are at a greater risk of the car toppling over.

Winds rarely blow at a consistent force and usually come in gusts. These gusts may leave you trying to overcorrect your course, which can cause you to change lanes and cause an accident.

If there are severe winds, it is best to avoid open roads, as winds are usually stronger in these areas.

COLD WEATHER

Preparing your vehicle for the ride is always best when driving in cold weather. Be aware of any warnings regarding heavy snowfall, add antifreeze to your car, and check there is enough tread on the tires for proper grip. Depending on where you live and the amount of ice, frost, or snow you get, you should have certain supplies in your car. These can include an ice scraper, de-icer, torch, phone charger, warm clothes, blankets, shovel, high visibility clothing, jump leads, fuel cans, food, drink, and warning triangles. You may need snow chains and sunglasses! Most of these are pre-cautionary, but it pays to be prepared.

Tip: In winter, ensure your windscreen fluid is topped up. Salt from the road can spray on your windscreen, and you may need to clean it frequently on your trip. Suppose you run out on the freeway (motorway). With the sun being lower in winter when it shines head-on - mixed with the salt residue, you will not be able to see the road or oncoming traffic.

HOT WEATHER

Unfortunately, hot weather also poses some form of risk when driving. You can prepare for the heat by stocking water bottles to avoid dehydration. Ensure your car's air conditioning system works optimally and keep your car tires, oil, and coolant levels topped up. It is also advised to avoid driving during the hottest times of the day because your car engine is at risk of over-heating. The last thing you'd want is to be stranded on the side of the road in the extreme heat.

So you now know how to calculate your car's budget and choose and find a great car. You have learned some great driving tips, but let's move on to the next chapter on how to look after your vehicle, so it stays reliable. There is a lot you can do yourself, and I will show you how - long term, this will save you money and leave you feeling more empowered and independent.

4

ESSENTIAL CAR CHECKS TO KEEP YOUR CAR RUNNING

"There's no freedom quite like the freedom of being constantly underestimated."

— SCOTT LYNCH

*N*ow that you know how to acquire a vehicle, you need to know how to take care of it. The reality is that cars need a lot of maintenance. You need to know the basics to avoid "calling someone" whenever a light on the dashboard turns on —or at least you need to know what the lights mean. From changing a tire to jump-starting a car and knowing when it needs to get serviced, it is time to take responsibility once the vehicle is in your possession. You also need to know what to do if you find yourself stranded on the side of the road with no help. Knowing what your alternative transport options are will keep you safe.

OWNERS MANUAL

You may not want to read the owner's manual, but trust me; it is the one thing that is sure to be your best friend. There are essential things that your user manual will tell you that you may not otherwise know when it comes to your car. First, it will tell you how to set up your car. Now, I know your car isn't the latest PlayStation console that requires a setup and login. Still, you need to know what features and options are available.

Beyond explaining how to turn the car ignition on and other setup details, your user manual will tell you how to use the radio, and headlights, connect wirelessly, and so much more. The user manual will describe any added or standard features of the car.

The user manual will also tell you when to take your vehicle in for maintenance checks, when changes need to be carried out, and at what intervals. Prevention is better than cure, and catching a problem sooner rather than later will save you money and a lot of inconvenience.

The manual will also tell you:

- The optimal octane fuel or gas level for your car
- What each of the dashboard warning lights means
- How to change the tires
- Your tire's ideal pressure
- Warranty information
- How to clean the vehicle inside and out

ESSENTIAL CAR CHECKS

There are some basic checks you are required to do. Some are needed more often than others.

FUEL: GAS (PETROL OR DIESEL)

Unfortunately, cars don't run on hopes and dreams, but it would be highly cost-effective if they did! Before you go on any trip, you need to make sure that there is enough fuel or gas in your car. You can usually tell by the gauge on the dashboard the fuel level in the tank. If you are only traveling a short distance and your tank is more than half full, you should be fine for your trip. A great rule of thumb is always to have enough fuel to get you to your destination and back home.

Tip: If still using traditional fuel such as gas (petrol or diesel) rather than electric, you can get a fuel container and fill it up for long-haul trips, just in case you are worried about running out; this is to get you to the nearest fueling station if needed.

Fuel: Electric

The same rule applies if you have an electric car. Plan your trip—research charge points on your route. There are now portable chargers that you can take with you that plug into the mains supply. But you need to check that you can do this at your destination. Ensure you can park close enough so the cable can reach and will they let you? Great if you can but have a backup plan just in case.

Oil

Next, you need to do an oil check. You can only top-up your oil if your car has a dipstick. Recently, some car manufacturers replaced the dipstick with an electronic sensor. (Autoaid, 2019). If your car only has the electronic sensor, it may be too complicated for you to top-up the oil yourself. Mercedes, BMW, Audi, and some Ford, Cadillac, Lincoln, Chevrolet, Chrysler, and Mazda models have removed the dipsticks from their new models, forcing the consumer to take their cars in for more servicing, and they also hope consumers will replace their vehicles more frequently. If you have one of these cars, get the garage to check the oil, and top it up if necessary every time it is in for a service to avoid the risk of having to book it in separately if the sensor light comes on. If your car still has a dipstick, this can save you money.

Ensure your vehicle is on a flat surface. Lift the hood (bonnet). The dipstick is often a different color, such as yellow, with an oil

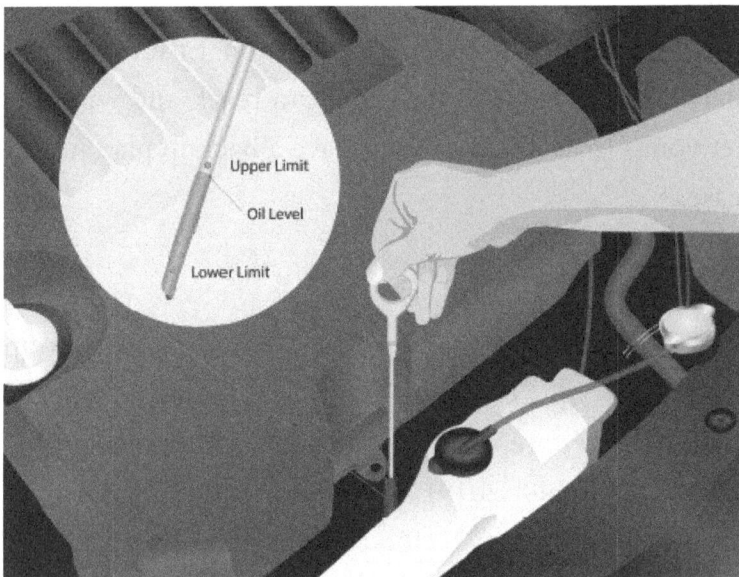

symbol. You will need a rag or cloth. Pull out the dipstick; it's long, like a fencing sword. Wipe off all the oil and look for the markings; there are two lines. The lower line (minimum mark) indicates that oil is too low if below this point.

The upper line is the max you should fill it. You want your oil level to be in-between these two lines. Sometimes "fill" may be written on the stick. Replace the wiped rod back into the oil, and pull it out again. This time check the oil level. If it is too low, you will need to top it up, and if you don't know what oil to use, your handy old owner's manual will tell you precisely what you need. You can also search online to find the right oil for your specific engine, make, model, and year of car. Be careful not to overfill with oil. Add a bit at a time and check it with the dipstick. Remember to wipe the dipstick before each test.

TIRES

You need to pay close attention to your tires. Not only should there be enough air in them, but you are checking for punctures, that the tread isn't smooth, and that there is enough thread on your tires to grip and keep you safe. Typically when tires are new, their tread depth is 10-11/32 inches (8-9mm). When the tread gets down to 4/32 inches (3mm), you need to check the tread monthly. When they reach 3/32 inches (2mm), you need to consider changing them.

Tread Depths

	Inches	mm
When bought New	10 - 11/32"	8 - 9
Good	7/32"or more	6 or more
OK	4 - 6/32"	*3 - 5
Replace soon	3/32"	2
Replace now/legal limit	2/32"	1.66

Inspect monthly when reach 3 mm

To check the tread depth, you can buy a tread depth gauge; they are not expensive. Cheaper still, you can use the edge of a coin.

In the US, you can currently use a penny, turn the penny so Lincoln's head faces down and place it in the tread. The distance from the edge of the penny to Lincoln's head is 2/32". If you can still see the top of Lincoln's head, you need to replace the tire.

In the UK, you can use a 20p coin. There is an outer band (border) on the coin. Place the coin in the tread. You must replace the tire if you can still see the outer band.

Don't just check one tire; check them all.

You may see faster wear and tear on individual tires for different reasons.

- Suppose your car is out of alignment or balance. Wear could be mainly seen on the side of a tire or heavily on the edges. When you replace your tires, as standard, ask the garage to align and balance them - this should help make the tread last longer on your new tires.
- If you over-inflate the tire, you will notice wear, mainly down the center.
- If wear is mainly on the tire's outer edges, you may have been driving with under-inflated tires.

To check the PSI (pounds per square inch) or BAR pressure needed, you can get this from the car's user manual, and it is also sometimes written on the inside of your car. A pressure amount is written on the tire, but this is usually the maximum PSI, not the optimal. Typically passenger cars can be between 32-35 PSI but check for your tire's optimal pressure. You can buy a tire pressure gauge to check the tire's pressure. A visual look at your tire is also a good indicator. Get used to how your tires look when you have just topped them up to their required level. You can also check and top up your car's tires at fueling (gas) stations. Sometimes there is a fee, and sometimes it's free; it is easy to do.

1. Know your tire's optimal pressure
2. Find your local station with an air dispenser.
3. Park close to the air dispenser so the long hose can reach all four tires.
4. Unscrew the cap which protects the valve off the first tire.
5. (a) If an **automated machine**: You may need to pay for the air; add your payment now. Then input your desired pressure value. You may hear the device start, and the pressure in the line is charged. Pick up the hose and attach it to the tire valve. There may be a lever on the hose attachment that you move down to lock the hose into place, which helps stop the air from leaking. The filling is likely to start immediately. The gauge is on the main machine; once the pressure you set is reached, the machine will beep. Release the lever and, remove the hose, replace the cap. (b) If an **older manual machine**: Pick up the hose and attach it firmly to the valve. There may be a lever on the hose attachment that you move down to lock the hose into place, which helps stop the air from leaking. There will be a manual trigger

to press to start the air. Hold this down for about ten seconds, watch the gauge on the hose, and then release the trigger. Repeat filling with air till the gauge reaches your desired pressure level. Once done, remove the hose, and replace the cap.

6. Repeat on the other three tires. **Tip:** You will have to stretch the hose either over the top of the car or around the side of it. They sometimes have a strong recoil and may pull away from you. Put your foot on it enough to hold it securely so you can get the hose fitted. Show it who's boss!

7. Replace the hose, ready for the next person.

Wiper Blades

You want to avoid getting caught in the rain with ineffective wiper blades. You need to be able to see clearly. Wiper blades need to be changed every year or two, but you shouldn't wait for a downpour to know if it needs changing. When you are in your driveway at home, squirt water using the levers on the side of your steering wheel used to clean your windscreen. When your wipers clear the water away, check how effectively they remove it. If the visibility is even slightly impaired, it may be time to change them.

Tip: If your wipers have an automatic setting, don't use it. If accidentally set off, the wipers can get damaged. Dry, dirty, and icy conditions are not the times to have your wipers set to automatic. If you want them on, switch them on.

WINDSHIELD-WIPER/WINDSCREEN-WASHER FLUID

You will use more windscreen fluid in winter, helping you clean away snow and salt. If it rains a lot where you live or whether you live in the city or the country, your windshield will need wiper fluid to help you see the road and keep the screen clean. The fluid is water and can be topped up with a bought screenwash. You can make a screen washer, which might be better for the environment, or you can shop around and find a cost-effective store-bought one.

COOLANT & ANTIFREEZE

To avoid your car overheating in the summer and to prevent it from freezing in the winter, you need to ensure your coolant and antifreeze levels are optimal. You may not necessarily lose any of these liquids as it is in a closed system, but sometimes these levels will need to be topped up. Refer to your manual for the specifics of your vehicle.

LIGHTS

Making sure all the lights are working perfectly, both front and back, is crucial for visibility and safety. When driving, it is essential to see and be seen. If a lightbulb is about to burn out, one of the dash lights that looks like a lightbulb may turn on to alert you. But every three months, when you have someone around, check your car lights by asking the other person to turn on different functions to see that the lights are working fine. They can turn the indicators on and off, press the brakes for you to check those lights work, and turn on the different headlights of your car as well.

AIR CONDITIONING

Suppose you live somewhere prone to warm or hot summers. In that case, you want to ensure that your air conditioning is optimal. When you send your car for a service, they can check the gas levels within your air conditioning system. If your garage can't do this for you, you will have to research somewhere that can.

GETTING YOUR CAR SERVICED

Getting your car serviced is like going to the doctor for a checkup, whether you are sick or not. It is essential, and it lets you know the health of your car so you don't face more significant problems later on.

In the UK, you must have a service and test done on your vehicle to obtain an MOT once your car is three years old. While requirements are less stringent in the US, sending your car for a service is far more than ensuring it is roadworthy.

Services are usually suggested yearly or at a particular mileage limit, whichever comes first. During service, the:

- Oil can be changed
- Air filters will be changed
- Spark plugs will be checked
- Brakes will be closely examined

Different aspects of your vehicle are checked at various services; chances are, after a certain period, these other aspects may need to be replaced and repaired. When you book your car for a service, you will provide the mechanic or dealership with the details of your vehicle, such as mileage, age of your car, and when the last service was. At that point, they will be able to give you a breakdown of the type of service they will be doing, the cost of the labor, and the parts for the service.

Taking your car for regular services (Hitchman, 2019):

- Improves the longevity of your car
- Enhances the safety of your car
- Extends your vehicle warranty
- Maximizes the car's value
- Ensures that different elements of your car are functioning optimally, especially the aspects that tend to be problematic more often

During a service, the mechanics may discover car parts that need replacing urgently or soon. So you may be facing additional costs to have this work carried out. Tell the garage beforehand that they should contact you before replacing them if they find new issues. Depending on your relationship with that garage, you may not trust them to give you the best price or believe these parts need replacing. You can source the parts yourself or get the repairs done elsewhere. Ensure you feel in control of the decision-making. There might not be an escape from the repairs, but at least you can control when the work is carried out and by whom.

Choosing a Garage for Service and Repair

Choosing the place that will take care of your vehicle is very important because you want to ensure that they will do a good job and that you will get good value for your money. When choosing a garage or auto repair shop, you may select one based on your parents' advice. If you are in an entirely new area, you may be unsure who to choose.

There are a few main factors that you want to take into consideration. You'll want to dig into the establishment's experience, how long they have been around, and what the tenure is of their mechanics. Next, speak to people in the area that you trust and ask them who their best recommendation would be. If you find a familiar name being dropped by many people, chances are, that is the place you should go. Check the online reviews of every potential establishment that you are considering. Next, pay a physical visit to each. Visiting allows you to do two things: see the establishment's condition, if it is clean and tidy, or if it seems like your car may get damaged while there, and get your quote. When you look at your first quote, you may not yet understand if the price is fair, but the more you "shop" around, the more you will get a better estimate of an expected and unrealistic price (Dowleys, 2017).

AFTER A CAR SERVICE

Once you have been to the auto repair shop or the garage, you are entitled to a written estimate and invoice of all costs, including details of parts and labor. You are also entitled to receive all the repaired and replaced parts. These parts will not only give you proof that new parts were put in your car, but if you ever need a second opinion on the work done or need to buy the parts yourself, you can easily do so. You have the right to inspect your car before leaving the garage, raise any questions, and return your vehicle if a warranty is issued and something seems amiss (City of Chicago, n.d.).

HOW TO CHANGE A TIRE

Whether you have seen someone else in distress or have been in this situation yourself, knowing how to change a tire can save you so much stress and anxiety because your tires are the one thing (or four things) constantly touching another surface.

Punctures and bursts can happen, and sometimes it isn't even your fault. The best way to be prepared for this scenario is first to have a spare wheel and, secondly, to know how to change the wheel.

Step one: First, ensure that you are pulled over in a safe place. It is better to drive on the flat wheel until you are somewhere safe than stay where your safety is compromised. Then you want to turn your hazard lights on whether it is daytime or nighttime. Wear a reflective vest and place your emergency triangle at the correct distance behind your vehicle (RAC, 2020).

Find a Safe Location & Place a
Warning Triangle

Turn On Your Hazard Lights

Step two: Get everyone out of the car (kept safely from traffic) and remove all the tools from the car's trunk, placing them next to you at the flat wheel. Removing the spare wheel just yet is unnecessary—you don't want it rolling out of your grasp and into the street. Ensure your car's handbrake is up and that you place a brick or a choke behind one of the tires that are still in good health (RAC, 2020). You don't want the car rolling.

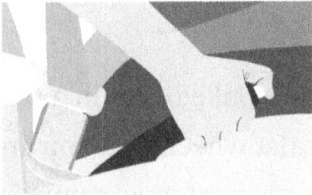

Apply the Parking Brake

Apply Wheel Wedges

Step three: Loosen the wheel nuts before jacking the car up. To prevent the wheel from turning while you are trying to loosen the nuts. Use the wheel spanner or lug wrench to loosen the nuts a fair amount, and remember, "righty tighty, lefty loosey" (RAC, 2020).

Loosen the Lug Nuts

Place the Jack Under the Vehicle & Raise the Vehicle with the Jack

Step four: Jack your car up.

There is a groove that will serve as a guide, usually located under the corresponding door of the wheel that is flat. Firmly place your jack in the groove and begin pumping or rotating, depending on how your jack works. Once your car is jacked all the way up and the wheel is entirely off the ground, you can fully loosen all the nuts and remove the tire. You must keep track of all nuts, spanners, and tools throughout the process so that nothing gets lost along the way (RAC, 2020).

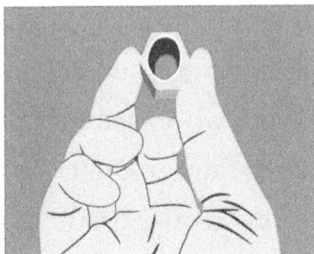

Unscrew the Lug Nuts

Remove the Flat Tire &
Take Out the Spare Tire

Step five: Mount the spare wheel in the same position where you removed the flat tire. Tighten the nuts with your fingers and then with the spanner or wrench. You are then going to lower the jack until the spare wheel is firmly on the ground and tighten the nuts as firmly as possible. After that, you will fully lower the jack and check the pressure of the spare wheel.

Mount the Spare Tire on the Lug Bolts

Tighten the Lug Nuts by Hand, then Lower
the Vehicle & Tighten the Lug Nuts Again,
after that Lower the Vehicle Completely

As long as the spare is not flat or damaged, you can drive it to your nearest gas station and fill the air in the spare tire (RAC, 2020).

After that, you need to take your tire to be repaired or replaced. It is essential to do this immediately. Ask the garage to do a wheel alignment to help keep your tire treads a little longer.

You should not drive without a spare wheel in your car. If you find yourself in the same situation the next day, but this time unprepared.

If you get a flat tire in the middle of the highway, it is important to slowly and gradually decrease your speed and move off the road with your hazard lights on. If your car breaks down on an eerily quiet and deserted road, do not get out of your vehicle. Instead, keep the doors locked and call someone for help.

BRAKES

Although your brakes will get checked on annual services or services every few thousand miles, it is vital to check them regularly. Suppose you hear noises or shudders in your car when you brake. Or have to press harder on the brake to get the car to stop - this could be because you are losing brake fluid. You need the garage to check your vehicle immediately if any of these problems occur.

HOW TO JUMP-START YOUR CAR

Imagine putting on the light in your car at night while getting your shopping out. You forget to switch it off, and the light stays on for hours. Because your vehicle is not running, the battery cannot charge and dies because of this light. Now, your car won't start, and you're stuck.

You can get your car started again by using jump leads or jumper cables and either connecting them to a vehicle with a fully functioning battery or using a battery-powered jump start kit.

To jump-start using another car, line both cars up to face each other (the other vehicle will need to be the one that moves into position). Ensure the handbrakes are on both cars and ignitions are off.

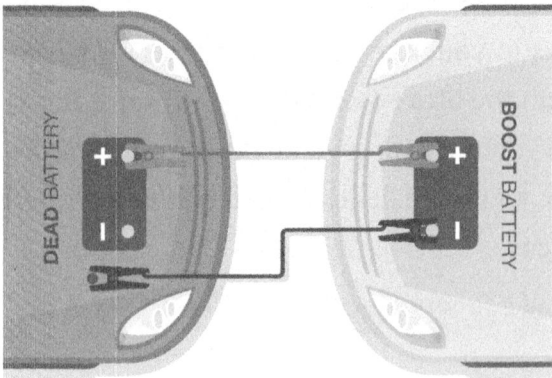

First, connect the red jump lead to both battery's positive terminals, starting with the working battery and moving on to the flat battery. Then connect the black lead cable to the negative terminals similarly. First, start the car with the working battery, leaving it to run for a few minutes, then start your car with the flat battery and leave both vehicles idle for 10 minutes. Make sure that no one touches any jumper cables when the vehicles are running. Turn off both cars, and disconnect the jump leads in reverse order starting with the black negative lead on your car. Ensure the leads don't touch each other.

Try to restart your vehicle and leave it idle for at least 10 minutes before driving. You should be all powered up after that point. (Automobile Association, 2020).

5

5

OTHER TRANSPORT OPTIONS AND BEING STREET SMART

"The standard you walk past, is the standard you accept."

— DAVID HURLEY

Depending on where you live, your need for a car may differ. For example, if you live a long way from the city and you must travel a long distance on your daily commute, you may not have access to public transport. Having your own car may be a necessity. There are pros and cons to having your own vehicle. The closer you live to a city, you may discover that it is more feasible to use public transport rather than to own your own car.

PUBLIC TRANSPORT VERSUS YOUR OWN TRANSPORT

Depending on where you live and where you are traveling, it is best to weigh the options; costs, efficiency, and time. Ideally, compare what suits you best and have a backup system for car or other transport issues, such as the buses in your area not running or whatever else may happen that prevents your mode of transport from working optimally.

While there are many benefits to having and using your own car, there are also several surprising benefits to using public transport. Not only is it better for the environment and overall congestion on the road, but you also have the unique opportunity to interact with people. You can read on your commute time rather than be stressed out by honking horns and the stress of driving, and you can save a lot of money (Rinkesh, 2017).

In the US, having your own vehicle is the most common solution for transportation because, outside of large cities, public transport can be disjointed and inefficient. But the US still has public transport solutions. For example, there are taxi cabs, Uber services, buses, trains, and airplanes for longer, cross-country trips.

Public transport is the most efficient way to get around the UK, especially in and around London. With public transport being so common in some areas, it is essential to know how to be safe when commuting on public transport. You need to know your exact route and your exits, stay where there are many people, and avoid quiet carriages. Stay out of unmarked or unlicensed cabs, and keep your valuables safe. Also, if you think something seems suspicious, report it, and trust your instincts (University College of London, 2020).

When you are using public transport, there are many payment options that you could use that could actively provide you with a discount for transportation services. Check what discounts may apply in your district or state and how much it could save you depending on how often you use public transport. For example, paying for monthly tickets or passes may be cheaper than purchasing daily for your commute. Suppose you are under a certain age or a student in full-time education. In that case, you will likely be eligible for a discounted price.

OTHER MODES OF TRANSPORTATION

Traveling and transportation are more than just getting from point A to point B. It is also about getting there safely and in the most comfortable way. Whether you have your own car or are used to taking an Uber. Always have more than one tried-and-tested method of transportation to get you to and from where you need to be. That way, if your car breaks down, you know which train to take, and you don't have to face the added anxiety of trying a new transportation method on top of getting your car fixed.

CYCLING

When talking about transport and vehicles, a very commonly forgotten form of transportation is cycling. It is cost-effective, good for your health, and a great way of gaining new insight into an area you have frequently traveled through with little thought. As long as it is done safely, you are good to go.

Whether experienced in cycling or entirely new to this form of transportation, it is always good to have some background info on getting started. There are many types of bikes to choose from, but if you only ride to and from work, you won't be going off-road too often. This means that there may be better options than a mountain bike. There are road bikes, utility bikes, electric bikes, and many more, but the choice has never been so good.

The cost of a bike will depend significantly on the quality of the cycle, whether it is new or secondhand,

and the intended uses. You will also need to take into account the fact that you will need safety gear and that you will need to do maintenance on your bike whenever the need arises.

Always plan your journey in detail, stay alert, and be aware of cars, pedestrians, and other cyclists on the road. Map your route out meticulously beforehand, wear the appropriate clothing, and lock your bike safely to prevent it from being stolen. If you feel unsafe at any point on your journey, it may be best to dismount from your bike and walk with your bike in hand.

MOPEDS (SCOOTERS)

Another form of transportation that is becoming extremely popular are mopeds. Mopeds provide almost all the benefits of using a bicycle without the sweat. Some run on battery power, some on gas or fuel. They are small and compact, easy to use, and highly cost-effective. Mopeds may be the way of the future. They are certainly the thing to have if you live in Italy. Not only are they cheap and easy on the environment, but they are also easy to maintain, safe, and easy to park and maneuver. Almost anyone can learn how to ride them.

A moped may be the best option for your travels if you have a short commute. For a student, it is an ideal form of transportation, and you may be able to ride it from one class to the next across campus. The minimum age to drive a moped is 16 in the UK, and you must pass Compulsory Basic Training (CBT). In the US, most states (not all) require you to have a license. You will also need to check the license class and minimum age requirements, as these both differ between states.

HOW TO READ A ROAD MAP

You may have thought this was never something you would have needed to consider. Google Maps provides straightforward and effective ways of giving users direction in a world that is almost constantly evolving. But there may be instances when you need access to an online map or GPS system, and you may only have access to a physical map. Knowing how to read a map is an integral part of geography and, yes, history as well.

Reading a road map, or any map for that matter, is relatively easy as long as you know a few things.

First, you need to know what the index means. To ensure that the map is not overcrowded with long words, general places of interest or special places may be marked with letters or numbers. These will be listed in the index, stating what each represents. For example, "A" might refer to a specific restaurant. Each index may have a different representation for different establishments. So it is always essential to briefly familiarize yourself with the index of the particular map you have in hand.

Next, you want to familiarize yourself with the legend of the map. The legend represents different elements, establishments, roadways, places of interest, and much more. For the most part, legends will consistently have the same symbols to represent the same items across a wide variety of maps. All train stations will look the same on a map, rivers will look the same, and so will other aspects. The legend is like a dictionary for you to know what the symbol on the map represents.

Lastly, you need to know the compass rose (showing the cardinal points N, S, E, W). This, accompanied by an actual compass, will tell you if you are heading in the right direction. If you have any scout experience, you can use natural elements like the sun to determine the direction that you're headed in.

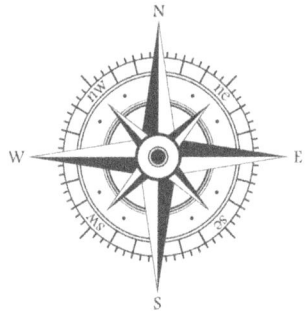

The scale of a map will tell you how large an actual area is and how much it has been shrunk to fit on the map.

Once you understand the map, you can plot your course from point A to point B. Through the scale, you could determine how far you'd have to travel. The legend will tell you what terrain you'd be traveling on, whether a road or a railroad, and you will know the general direction you would be traveling in.

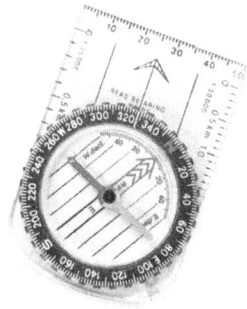

Map reading is an essential skill often taught on school trips and deemed necessary for education. But as the world becomes more digital, maps and GPS tracking services are readily available on our phones. You may not have an immediate need to read a map. Still, for the most part, it is a handy skill to have and fulfilling when you discover you can navigate your way without any electronics. It is also helpful if you vacation in a remote place where GPS and phone signals are not readily available. You may need to become more familiar with the local languages in places like this. Knowing how to read a map can make your holiday a pleasant experience. If all else fails and you can access it, you can always head to Google or Apple Maps to find your way home.

STAYING STREET SMART

There are general safety rules that you should follow when you are in your car's driver's seat.

- Never pick up strangers or hitchhikers. We have all seen way too many horror movies, so we know better. Avoid this at all costs unless it is someone you know and if you are accompanied by two other people.
- Always ensure that someone is expecting to meet you at your destination. If you don't arrive for any reason, that person can call for help or actively seek you out.
- Fully charge their phone battery. You don't want to be in a sticky situation with no way of calling for help or alerting someone that you will be late.
- Someone is aware of your location. Technology has provided us with fantastic features on social media and apps that can be used for safety purposes. Sending your live location to a friend or family group means that those closest to you know exactly where you are at any given point. You don't have to use your phone while driving.

- Always carry some cash. If you face car trouble you can't fix, help cannot get to you fast enough. You can call a cab, a taxi, or even an Uber to immediately get you to a safe place.

ALWAYS STAY "STREET SMART" AND BE AWARE OF YOUR SURROUNDINGS.

In an ideal world, you wouldn't need to be street-smart. Street-smart is defined as "having the ability to stay safe and survive the dangers and difficulties we face daily."

Talking to strangers and sensing you are in a potentially threatening situation are ways that force us to be street smart. Whether you already thought you were street-smart or not, being street-smart doesn't just apply to a street per se, but it does mean keeping yourself safe in all public settings.

- It means ensuring you aren't followed and keeping your thumb on an emergency dial if you walk alone.

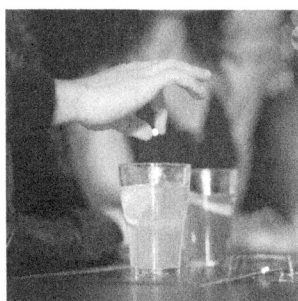

- Keep an eye on your drink in public areas. Some bars provide covers for glasses or bottles to stop people from spiking/drugging them.

- Don't accept drinks from strangers; they may have drugged it.
- Never keep all your money in the same place. Split your money up and keep some separate (enough to get you home), in a zipped pocket, for example, just in case something happens to your wallet or the money in it. Then you have it if you need a taxi home.

To stay street-smart, you need to be;

- Aware of your surroundings. If you are in a parking lot alone at night.
- Don't be distracted by looking down at your phone.
- Check your surroundings. Is anyone else present? Are there any people that look suspicious? How far is it from where you are to your closest exit point?
- Don't get into cars with strangers or unmarked or unlicensed taxis. This is the same as getting in the car with a stranger.
- When alone in public, walk confidently, even if you may not feel brave. If you look like someone people shouldn't mess with, chances are they won't mess with you. Also, suspicious

people will try to intimidate you. Don't allow yourself to be intimidated. If someone is making you feel uncomfortable, be bold and assert yourself. Please make a point of loudly telling them to back off. It is essential to know that you should never be afraid to cause a scene if you feel unsafe and don't show any signs of weakness.

- You could also carry a safety device if walking alone is unavoidable. There are alarms, whistles, lights, and sprays which you can keep in your hand while walking.
- If walking to your car, ensure you have your car key ready. It helps to have a small torch on your keyring.
- Lastly, keep yourself from being easily distracted. Keep focus and know when to leave in a potentially harmful situation. Whether it is a social group that is getting too rowdy or a date that has suddenly had an atmosphere shift, making you feel highly uncomfortable.

Ideally, you'd want to avoid risky situations altogether. But we don't live in a constantly and consistently safe world. So as much as you try to avoid dangerous situations, you need to know how to safely remove yourself from one should you find yourself in that position.

- The first thing to do is always **trust your gut**. You may get an inclination in the pit of your stomach that something feels off long before you spot the suspicious behavior. It's like noticing when someone is sad or upset by their body language. We sense things that extend beyond our usual frame of reference. So when you get a clue that something doesn't feel right, trust yourself and leave.

- If you cannot remove yourself from the situation, it is vital to be **seen and heard**. Do not be afraid to cause a scene if someone makes you uncomfortable. If someone is following you while walking in a mall, head to a busy area like the food court and speak out. Head straight to security and point the person out. Tell people all around you, even if they are strangers, that you are feeling unsafe. Younger children are advised to approach a mother who has a child with her. Causing a scene can keep you safe. On that same point, do not be afraid to scream and yell. Screaming draws attention to you and prevents suspicious people from getting away with crimes quietly.

- If your purse or phone is snatched, **yell and scream**, and someone may stop the criminal. In a world that tries to silence victims, be as loud as you can be for yourself and others.

- This leads me to my next point—**help others** if they approach you in situations of discomfort. If you see someone being picked on or bullied, or if you see someone being the target or a victim, speak out immediately and seek help. Don't approach a crowd single-handedly. Instead, get someone to help you when you see someone in a difficult situation with many people. Everything that you would do to keep yourself safe does the same to keep others safe. While you continue to remain kind and helpful, **stay cautious, too**. People may see your goodness as a weakness but stand your ground. If the situation looks dangerous, then seek help immediately and remain vigilant.

There are many other ways that you can stay safe and ways that you can protect yourself. Consider taking a **self-defense class**, which is an excellent way to keep fit and safe.

6

FIND YOUR CAREER PATH

"I always wanted to be somebody, but now I realise I should have been more specific."

— LILY TOMLIN

*C*ongratulations if you are lucky enough to know what you want to do for a career. I wish I'd had direction at your age. If you do know, though, you are the exception. Most of us still need to discover who we are, what we enjoy doing, what drives us, and what our strengths are. But fear not! You can take steps to better understand all these factors and gain clarity on what you might succeed at. So do not panic.

There are benefits to having an idea of what you want to do the younger you are. Whether you are 15, 18, 21, or

31, it is always beneficial to gain insight to aid you in discovering your path and even reimagining your future.

Having an idea of the path you wish to take can help you make aligned choices. You can be more informed on which elective (optional) subjects at school and college to take. Which out-of-school activities, work experience, or internship opportunities to apply for. This also, in turn, helps you avoid having a zig-zag-looking resume or CV with no direction. Instead, you could have focused experience and an aligned education, pointing like an arrow directly to the job or jobs you planned for.

Occasionally, someone with a zig-zagging breadth of knowledge and resume will get the job. Sometimes, this can be beneficial and add value, but this is the exception, not the rule!

You want to avoid too many non-starters, such as dropping out of the wrong courses, moving industries, or constantly re-training. Recruiters will ask why you have changed industries or direction. The more you appear not to be serious about; their industry, the available position, or show career stability generally, the less likely they will be to hire you. I wasted a lot of time. I did more than zig-zag - I catapulted myself off the page! If you want to be the arrow - let me show you how!

Step 1. Get to Know Yourself

How you enjoy spending your time and what's important to you can indicate what you want to do for work. Try not to think about things you are passionate about, as that usually doesn't give you the best foundation to build. Still, it's nice to have a job that will put a spring in your step when you wake in the morning (Coursera, 2022).

FIND YOUR PATH - EXERCISE

So with that in mind, think about the following questions and write a few notes about each. Use a notebook, not a scrap of paper. You need to keep these notes to refer back to and build upon.

What are you interested in?

1. Think of things you enjoy learning about.
2. When you have time, what do you enjoy doing?
3. Which do you prefer, more physical or mental work?
4. Which do you like best, working indoors or outside?

What are your values?

1. What is most essential in your life?
2. What priorities do you have in your life?
3. What makes you feel like you have meaning or purpose?
4. Are there any changes needed that are important to you?

What traits are essential to you?

1. Success, what does that look like to you?
2. If you could have more of something, what would that be?
3. Are there any of your strengths that you enjoy?
4. Of your skills which makes you the proudest?

Once you have a list for the above, move on to step 2.

Step 2. What Motivates You?

Let us look at your motivations for working. Are you wanting a high-paid job straight off the mark, or are you looking to work at your preferred choice of employer regardless of the first salary offer? Would you like to dress smart for the office and enjoy some office banter, or are you keen to work from home? There is usually a compromise, especially with your first few roles. So it's essential to prioritize what is most important to you.

Here is an example list of some priorities. Jot down your list of priorities. You can use these or add your own. What will be most important to you?

- Money
- Benefits
- Career growth
- Location
- Flexibility
- Autonomy
- Work/life balance

Step 3. Ten Years from Now!

Consider your long-term goals. Personally and professionally - where do you want to be in 10 years? Do you expect a six-figure salary, a fast-track route to top-level management, be an editor at a prestigious publishing house, or be one of the first chosen for the human-crewed mission to Mars (the planet, not the chocolate confectioner, although that sounds awesome too!)? Write down what you want your long-term goals to be. Then consider researching companies that look to provide you with what you are looking for or match the growth you hope to achieve. Are they looking to develop managers or increase automation? Are they expanding as a company, advertising their long-term growth plans?

Step 4. Career Aptitude Testing, *including* Strength Tests

There are many free and paid career aptitude tests online. Complete a minimum of two and compare the results. Try to answer the questions honestly without overthinking what your answer means. For example, you want to avoid picking the answers you think will lead to the career you want to see in the results. Instead, you need to be honest (be yourself) with what you like, what you prefer, and what you think. These answers will give a much more helpful output that you can take away and process. These tests often identify and highlight your strengths. This might be the first time you have seen them noted down. Also, it's worth understanding that these algorithms used in the testing are a measure of your strengths today. Your strengths and weaknesses are not set in stone. As you expand your experiences and push outside your comfort zone, you will have many opportunities to grow and discover that you have developed new strengths.

The idea of these tests is not to give you a definitive answer and career. But to highlight some possible professions based on your honest answers, interests, and current strengths. (If you have seen the movie Divergent, you will know you don't have to pick what has been chosen for you, you get to choose what you want!) These tests show you more career options than you might have previously considered. More than just the box-standard generic roles; nurse, fireman, lawyer, or accountant, but careers you may have yet to hear of, ones in-between and adjacent. So treat it as part of the research of getting to know who you are and what is available, and add the results to your notes.

Here are some career aptitude sites (inc. strengths) I found, but there are many others:

- Career Fitter
- Truity
- Career Hunter
- Brain Manager

Note: these sites state that the tests are free to take, but sometimes there may be a small fee to see the results or subscribe to their services for extended periods. Just so you are aware.

- Myers-Briggs (myersbriggs.org)

Myers-Briggs is a personality test often used by both individuals and businesses alike. This test is not free but widely used. There is a free version that works similarly 16personalities.com, which you could also try.

Step 5. Sectors

Next up, consider the type of sectors that exist. Working environments within different sectors can differ along with their business priorities. Some may align better than others with your goals.

So, what sectors do I mean?:

- Private sector - a privately owned company looking to profit and grow. Typically their business model has growth potential, more opportunities, and bonuses. But it can be a competitive environment.
- Public sector - you would work for a government-run (US - local, state, or federal. UK - National) business. This sector includes public health care and public safety programs. These jobs can be much more stable, flexible in hours, and typically less stressful.
- Non-Profit (includes charities) - these businesses exist out of a public need. Their priority is to fulfill a goal or purpose. The benefit of working for a non-profit is that it can bring meaning to your life. Staffing is often less, so you may have more responsibility and gain experience more quickly.

Step 6. Industries

Like sectors, consider the different industries. Look for established industries and see if their goals fit yours.

Some industries include; energy, telecommunications, consumer goods, agriculture, media, construction, finance, and e-commerce. Search the internet as there are many more. Find some that look interesting to you. Once you have a few in front of you, research what roles they are advertising for, promotion opportunities, and whether the industries are growing or declining.

Tip: Independent research is also regularly carried out on what jobs will be most needed in the next five to ten years. You only need to ask your search engine. Suppose you like the city where you live. Research what opportunities will be available in the next few years. Are they forecasting a requirement for more programmers or coders? Look for what there will be a demand for. You could position yourself perfectly. There may be an industry that matches your criteria, and a bonus if there will be many vacancies once you are qualified and job searching!

Step 7. Other Resources

It is also worth considering professional resources.

- Career Centers - your college, university, or town sometimes have career centers to provide resources and offer advice and support. They can discuss where you are now and your options to get on the path you are interested in. Utilize these services. They are there for you!
- Career Coach - this would cost you a fee, but professionals do this for a living. Ensure you do a background check on them first to ensure they are what you need.
- Mentor - having a mentor is perfect for every step of your career. Is there someone at college or a professional that you know and admire? It could be worth approaching them and asking for their advice. This works particularly well if they have experience in the industry you are interested in. Mentoring is free, although you can chat over a coffee you pay for.

Step 8. Research Options

With all your notes in front of you, you will start to get a more holistic picture of yourself. Start researching careers and industries that could be a good fit for you.

When you write down all the options, note which priority, value, interest, etc., that option addresses. Pay attention to those roles that address your highest priorities.

LET'S LOOK AT YOUR LIST MORE CLOSELY

With your list of exciting careers in front of you, let's explore them a little further.

(a) Research job openings.

Look on job sites for either current or old job vacancies in your area. Look at the responsibilities and other details, such as the type of person they are looking for, particular strengths, or other skills and interests. Check against all your notes. Do any of the roles fit most of your requirements? How do you feel when you think about each of these career options? Can you see yourself in any of these roles? Some websites you can use include; Linkedin, Indeed, and Monster.

(b) Company reviews

Use websites to learn about the companies you are interested in. Look for reviews on the company and industry. Glassdoor is a good site for this. Also, carry out further research on the industry you are considering. Pay attention to what current and past employees say and any current issues within the industry.

(c) Information gathering interviews.

Reach out to anyone connected with the company you are interested in. This could be someone you know who works there, has worked there, or someone who knows someone. What information can they provide about the role? If you are on Linkedin, you can see if any of your contacts are connected to someone who currently works at a company you are interested in. If it's appropriate, reach out to your friend and see if they can help you get the information you need. Can they make an introduction?

NEXT STEPS

Whether you are getting ready to leave college or are still in high school, this may be the first time it's really sunk in that you will be a fully functioning independent career person. Weirder still, you have researched ideas about what that looks like and what you might be doing. You have also got to know yourself a little better. Who knew you had hidden strengths? I did, and now you do too!

Your next steps depend on where you are now compared to what you need as entry requirements for the careers and roles you are interested in. Figuring out and plotting the best course is the easy bit. There are people that can help you, including your tutors, career advisors, and career centers. Sticking to the plan and putting in the effort is all up to you.

Once you know which university, course, or career you want to pursue, you can establish what grades, SAT scores (US), or experience you require for entry. These need to be goals in your plan. In the next chapter, I will show you how to create SMART goals and ace college.

7

HOW TO ACE COLLEGE, SET SMART GOALS, AND DEVELOP YOUR CRITICAL THINKING

"The elevator to success is out of order. You'll have to use the stairs, one step at a time."

— *JOE GIRARD*

*E*veryone wants to be a great exam taker, do their best at school, and constantly put their best foot forward. But sometimes, you need a little extra nudge and motivation. You may feel overwhelmed by looming exams or assignments you are expected to complete. Rest assured that our minds tend to focus on the negative and the worst possible outcome we can expect. We use this as a survival tactic. You can't be surprised if you constantly expect the worst. I will help you surprise yourself in the best possible way.

Let's look at how you can ace your classes at school and college and learn how to set goals.

Before we jump into how to ace college, It's important to understand why education is important to you. I advise everyone to try their best at school and college for 9 fundamental reasons.

9 REASONS WHY EDUCATION IS VITAL

1. Knowledge: Education isn't just about passing exams. It forms part of the knowledge building blocks for you to become a new valuable member of society. Learning from our history also prepares us to become responsible citizens. (a) You take over the family business, and the commercial understanding and skills you gained from your business studies course become invaluable. (b) Your persuasive writing skills learned in English convince local politicians to make improvements in your area. (c) Your Spanish lessons help you communicate with someone in trouble and danger when no one else can get through to

them. The more we know, the more we can contribute.

2. Regret: Gaining excellent grades will naturally open doors for you. But if you don't try and give your best while in education, you may learn to regret it later.

3. Gives you choices. Poor grades give you fewer career options. Completing and doing well in high school will then provide you choices in higher education, apprenticeships, and scholarships. It may also give you the grades and scores for entry into prestigious universities.

4. Quality of life. Learning should be fun and interesting. Knowledge expands and improves our minds. It, in turn, feels good, which builds confidence and self-esteem.

5. Cost: Suppose you decide later to go back to college and redo or gain new qualifications. In that case, this can be very costly. As an adult, you may have to juggle work, friends, and even children - this takes enormous commitment, trust me!

6. Habit building. Applying yourself and working hard at school and college builds habits in other parts of your life, such as demonstrating a great work ethic.

7. You raise your standards. You learn a lot about yourself when challenged. Once you experience what you are capable of and see that you are capable of many great things, you will take this standard forward in many aspects of your adult life.

8. Qualifications are ever-lasting: No one can take your education away from you. Finishing high school opens doors, and college and university open many more.

9. You are more likely to earn more if you gain a higher education qualification.

Not so many years ago, people had one job for life. One employer for most of their careers. Today it's common to move around every 2-3 years, either up through promotion or to another company. Because we are more fluid, qualifications, experience, and how we look on paper are vital so we can market and promote ourselves with each move and progression. So give yourself the best shoo-in to adulthood and stick in at school. Because you're worth it and deserve it.

HOW TO ACE YOUR CLASSES

Understand upfront that you can only do your best. But your best can be outstanding. We all have different backgrounds and different things going on in our lives. You may feel you are on an unequal starting block to your peers and even may feel left behind. But know that you bring unique strengths with you, personally, academically, and professionally you can achieve the same, if not more, than most of your peers. I will show you how. Regardless of where you are now, know it is always possible to turn things around. At some point, most things holding us back become excuses. Believe me when I say the driver of your success is you. You make it happen. You need these 3 simple elements:

- You have to really want it
- Be prepared to work hard
- Don't give up, be persistent

Working toward an academic goal is more than just a one-and-done deal. It takes persistent hard work to obtain the desired result. The tips that I am going to give to you need to be done consistently. It is not a solution to help you just this semester or this year, but rather one that will help you throughout your academic career.

WHEN AT SCHOOL, COLLEGE & UNIVERSITY

- **No Distractions in Class**. The first thing you will do is find a place to sit in class where you are not easily distracted. Whether away from your friends or the person you find extremely attractive, choose a spot where your focus cannot be easily pulled. Trust me, real friends will understand.

- **Be Prepared**. When you head into class, you want to be prepared and ready for the purpose of the class—which is to learn. This means having all the materials you need for class, such as; notebooks and pens. Ensure you have your textbooks, study-notes, and be mentally prepared to take in information. Something fundamental is preparing for your classes the day before. Most high school and college classes give you a detailed outline and breakdown of the content your teacher or lecturer hopes to cover each day or week. While it is safe to assume that the only time you cannot fully prepare for a class is on the very first day. Set time aside to review freshly taught concepts every day after that. Read over concepts covered the next day. If you don't understand something or a topic is challenging to grasp, make a note of it and query it with your educator the next day in class, don't wait or risk falling behind.

- **Take Notes**. Next, you will take as detailed notes as your hands allow. Considering that taught content is usually built upon one lesson upon the previous lesson, any gap in knowledge or information could leave you struggling to grasp new concepts. Ensure you take detailed notes to know where you need more information. This leads me to the next point…

- **Ask Questions**. I'm sure you have heard that there is no such thing as a stupid question, and I am sure that you could think of at least 10 deliberately dumb questions to ask to prove me wrong. And while that is done in good jest, it is often found that when you think something is a stupid question, others who had the same question also think it was dumb and choose not to raise their hands. By being the hero and asking the question, the entire class received clarity. Remember, educators get paid to answer your questions. Please don't be shy to utilize them!

- **Contribute in Class**. It is always a great idea to contribute to class discussions. I remember once in a class where a teacher was explaining a concept that was difficult to understand. One of the quiet guys who sat at the back of the class raised his hand and presented an analogy that he thought best described the concept. He asked the teacher if his analogy was correct. It was right; the whole class used his analogy to understand the concept and used it in the run-up to the exam. Please share your thoughts and ideas because your thoughts, if correct, may be the tool people use to understand what is being taught. Contributing to class also goes far beyond your understanding and sharing of ideas. Many courses may give you extra credit or points that count toward participation. Imagine what a difference 5% may make to the mark you end up with at the end of the semester.

- **Technology and Social Media**. Lastly, in class, you want to keep your phone, social media, or online shopping apps on your computer neatly tucked away to avoid distraction. The reality is that cell phones serve as one of the biggest distractions, and if it rings in the middle of class, it may bother everyone else. Make sure it is silent and packed away in your backpack to avoid your automated response immediately responding to texts. Beyond your phone, consider that many people take lecture notes on their laptops. This, too, can be a distraction and cause you to wander onto the internet. Be sure to remove distractions from your computer as well.

Many high school students put in the minimum effort: they turn up - the educator teaches - they listen - job done! But that is just the tip of the iceberg in terms of what commitment and effort are needed.

Regarding the effort needed to succeed, think of the 80:20 rule here. The educators provide you with your syllabus, teach the lessons, and provide reference material. If you have questions, they provide answers. They also mark your work. That is 20%. You need to bring 80%. It's not just the time spent being present and listening in class. It's also the prep and study time unseen by others, but it needs to happen. Think of the effort required like an iceberg, with the crux of your effort happening unseen, outside the visible scheduled class time. With commitment, organization, and balance, you can do this.

THE ICEBERG ILLUSION

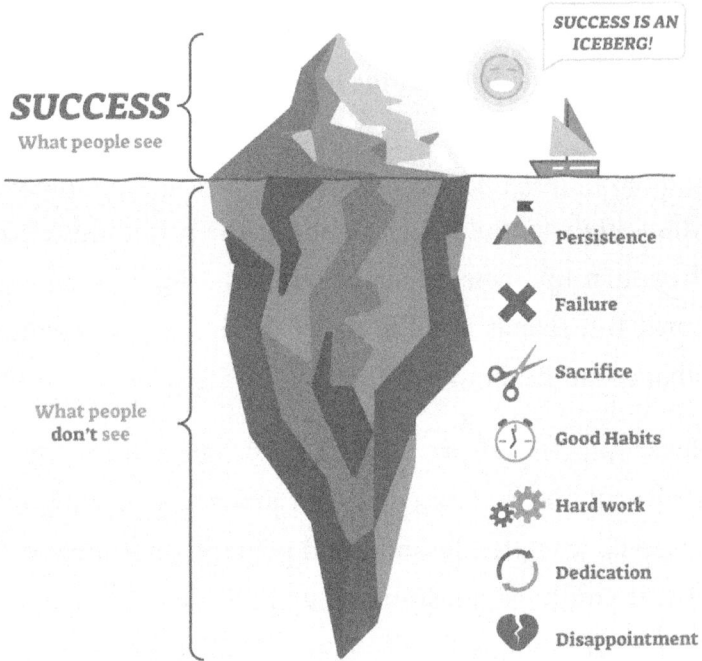

SUCCESS IS AN ICEBERG!

SUCCESS
What people see

What people
don't see

Persistence

Failure

Sacrifice

Good Habits

Hard work

Dedication

Disappointment

WHEN AT HOME

It would help if you had a desk or table at home to help you get organized and study. If you have a desk, clean it if it's hidden under piles of stuff, and make it a nice place to work. Have everything you need for your study session; adequate lighting and a wall planner to track when work is due. Make it comfortable to work - but not too comfortable that you fall asleep! Having a dedicated study space is essential. This is where your brain will be trained to be the most effective and get the most work done. You will ideally have no distractions (a no-phone zone). If you can't study at home, find a library or somewhere else quiet and conducive to study that you can go to regularly. Try to use the same spot each time. Your brain gets used to your surroundings and immediately knows you are in study mode. It makes quite the difference. Music through headphones may help, do that as long as it's not too distracting. The same tracks can also induce your study mode quicker. Your brain is pre-programmed to switch to this mode when it hears it. Headphones or music are also an excellent tool to block unwanted distracting back-ground sounds which are out of your control.

STUDYING & EXAMINATION PREPARATION

Part of acing your class means appropriately preparing and passing your examinations. This is an excellent way to ensure you set yourself up for success. You see, the foundation you have laid in the above steps means that you have already done most of the job successfully. We want to continue with success by building on the existing knowledge and studying what we have already learned.

The first thing you are going to do is plan when to study. By planning and setting aside time dedicated to studying, you allow yourself to cover content stress-freely without cramming all your work in two weeks before your final exams. Plan in time to complete homework and review notes and concepts, not just time for revision. Having a schedule helps with studying and will enable you to keep track of assignments and due dates. Please take notice of these critical dates by planning them. The aim of academic institutions is not to catch you off guard, even though it may seem this way when you are facing intense exam stress and it feels like the world is against you. If you are fully aware of tests and assignments and are well-prepared for these aspects and components of the course, you will find yourself ready for exams. Stick to your study plan; your revision time will then consist of perfecting answers (to maximize grades or scores) rather than cramming concepts.

CAPTURE, CONTROL, PLAN & EVOLVE

Next, you may adopt the capture, control, plan, and evolve method. This method tells us to:

1. Capture your obligations as a student—what needs to be done, when it needs to be done, and what do you need to get it done? Make the list of your obligations as detailed as possible, even if it is something like returning a textbook to the library.

2. Control your time by making an extremely detailed schedule. Every hour of the day should have something assigned to it. More important than planning the schedule is sticking to it.

3. Plan your study time. Some work is consistent and needs to be done almost daily. Studying is more sparsely spread out. If you dedicate a day to studying, stick to it.

4. Evolve with your study tactics. Studying—how you take in information—and your schedule are living organisms constantly adapting. Next week, something new may come up, and you may have to rearrange your entire study schedule. This is normal to continuously work optimally. Be willing and able to adapt as and when you need to.

Tip: You may find it easier and quicker to learn new information as soon as you get home. So rearrange your tasks, so the most taxing is first. Leaving it till late at night will mean you are tired, making it more demanding and taking longer. Spending an additional half hour in the morning re-reading new information will also help embed it.

PROCRASTINATION

The challenge I found myself facing, and have seen others face, is that we are often unprepared for our exams. Not because we were watching TV or heading out with our friends every night. But because we focused on completing other aspects of our coursework, working, cleaning, or simply not wanting to think about exams yet. Studying wasn't urgent at the time, and exams seemed far away.

And so, studying gets postponed for things that seem more urgent. Eventually, you are panicking because the exam is only a couple of months away, and you haven't sufficiently studied. There are also other reasons why people find themselves avoiding or postponing studies. They may not enjoy the subject, they may not like the lecturer or the teacher, the class may be too exhausting, or they may be focused on other courses. Avoid procrastination, and push through the first five minutes of study. The first five minutes are the most challenging.

"Believe you need to understand and remember all the elements of your subjects throughout the year.."

Find your stride. Focus on achieving a great pass, and believe you need to understand and remember all the elements of your subject throughout the year, not just in the run-up to exams. Remember, if you don't understand an aspect of your coursework, address it at the time and make extra notes and examples. The run-up to exams is best spent fine-tuning your answers to maximize your grades."

Tip: To help avoid procrastination, do this.

- Plan what you will study, so you can get straight into it
- Set a time block
- Commit to completing the task, prioritize it
- Do the bit you find hardest first
- If you complete it, you can reward yourself afterward

You can also do this:

- Tidying your desk the night before, ready to go
- Have a picture or item on or near your desk that inspires you to study, a goal perhaps
- Put headphones on with your study tracks to get you focussed quicker and block out other sounds - get in the zone!
- Tell those that will distract you you need, i.e., an hour to study uninterrupted.
- Remember no cell (mobile phones), put on silent or switch off.

STUDY BUDDY (STRAIGHT AS)

Another way you can work toward your success is by finding a study partner who obtains straight As. They will help you focus on what's important and understand complex concepts. Also, they will be someone to whom you are accountable—no space for slipping grades because your friend is going to be on your back!

COMPLETE PAST EXAM PAPERS

When you are studying for exams, there are some tips and tricks that you can use to make sure you are prepared and ready. The best trick is to complete past examinations and adhere strictly to the exam paper's time limit and requirements. You can then get feedback from your professors or higher-performing peers and see areas of improvement in your work.

Unfortunately, most of us learn late that studying is more than just reading and memorizing content or rewriting the same notes repeatedly until you have memorized them word for word. While these methods help you remember concepts in a parroted fashion, you must ensure you understand the work you are trying to learn. This means not only knowing the concepts but also being able to apply them in practice.

Teach Someone Else

Another trick to ensure you understand a concept you have studied is paraphrasing it and trying to explain it to someone else. If you can keep the concept's meaning while using your own words, you have successfully grasped the idea.

The Value of Sleep

There is a reason why we spend a third of our lives resting and rejuvenating. Your mind cannot optimally function when tired. Creating a vicious circle where we catch up on studying by working late into the night. We are too exhausted to focus on our exams, we get bad marks, and so we try to catch up on studying again by working late into the night. Avoid pulling all-nighters when trying to study; effective time management is the best way forward.

Relationships With Teachers, Lecturers, and Professors

Maintaining an excellent professional relationship with your professors or teachers is extremely important. Of course, you aren't hoping to be a teacher's pet, but you want to set a good impression and put your best foot forward.

Knowing what your lecturer's expectations are from their students is essential. Two people can lecture the exact same course with the same content. Still, their personalities may incline them to present the course-work and content in different forms. It is, therefore, always best to know what you and your peers are expected to do.

Always be sure to hand assignments and projects in on time and to do the requirements set by your lecturer. Be aware of your teacher's consultation times. These times are for you to schedule a meeting with them, ask questions, or air concerns about the course content. This is an excellent way of gaining clarity on concepts you may need help understanding, even for raising questions if you are uncomfortable asking in front of the whole class (Taylor, 2021).

OTHER TIPS FOR SUCCESS

If you have planned your study time and stuck to it, you need time to step back and check for balance. Add regular exercise to your schedule. It doesn't have to be extreme sports or high-impact but could include walking or cycling to college. Joining a friendly soccer (football) match on the weekend might be fun and a great way to make new friends. Do fundamentally different activities to give your brain and sometimes your eyes a break. Do something you enjoy as a hobby, or treat yourself to something. You have been working hard. It's great to get outdoors as you will need vitamin D if you have been working the whole time indoors. Give yourself time-out in whatever shape or form lets you reset. Don't skip this! All your other efforts will be more efficient if you allow yourself this time. I can't stress this enough.

SETTING SMART GOALS

"Setting goals is the first step in turning the invisible into the visible."

— TONY ROBBINS

In the real world, you need to have goals. You need to set goals about what you want to achieve, personally, professionally, and academically. It would help if you had goals dedicated to the person you aspire to be. Do you want to change your mindset? Do you want to be kinder and more empathetic?

Once you have your goal set out, the hard part is actually achieving that goal. Having your goal written down on paper and looking daily at it is a great reminder.

Still, that reminder is futile if you don't set plans to achieve those goals.

You should set and establish SMART goals at any point in your life. You can't just say you want to get straight As as a goal. Yes, that is the first step—knowing what you would like to achieve—but setting a goal isn't just about setting a goal. When you establish a goal, you have a destination you hope to work toward. After that, you must plan the exact route to get to that destination. You will define what car you will take and note what snacks you want to bring along for the ride.

While this is just a metaphor, it is the truth. You need to have a goal in mind, which is the first step, and then you need to have a detailed method on how, when, and why you will achieve this goal.

This is why you have to set SMART goals. SMART stands for: Specific, Measurable, Attainable, Relevant and Timely.

All the aspects you need to include when creating and establishing your goal.

So while achieving straight As is a goal, it is not a SMART goal per se - well, not yet! Before we unpack this example, you need to ask yourself if your goal aligns with where you are currently. For example, you would only be setting this goal if you were a student, and you wouldn't set this goal if you were failing most of your subjects. If you were failing, you might aim for Cs. But if you are currently a C or B student, hoping to achieve straight As is a realistic goal.

Let's unpack it. You would start with the objective of the goal, which is that you'd like to achieve As in math, English, and science (specific). Next, you will state that you hope to achieve this goal by the end of the semester or by the end of the academic year (measurable). You will make the goal of attaining As in three subjects as opposed to six because this is more achievable and more realistic than putting pressure on yourself (attainable). You are focusing on these subjects because you may be hoping to get into a math or science course in college (relevant). You will set a deadline for when you are hoping to achieve this goal (timely).

Now that you have a SMART goal achieving it will be more manageable and realistic.

ANALYTICAL SKILLS & CRITICAL THINKING

In a work environment, analytical skills can include effectively communicating analysis, thinking creatively and critically, analyzing data, and researching.

Critical thinking helps you understand a situation, notice and predict outcomes, organize and process the facts and other information, and make conclusions. This could be to define the problem and develop solutions to resolve it.

There are ways that you can improve your analytical and critical thinking skills (Indeed Editorial Team, 2021):

- Reading more
- Building your math skills
- Playing games that challenge your brain: Scrabble, Checkers, Chess, Cluedo, brain-game apps, and logical games
- Learning a new skill
- Being observant
- Respectfully debating
- Exercising daily to improve brain functionality

- Journaling
- Being curious
- Improve your deductive reasoning

A deductive reasoning challenge could be:

(a) Look at several potential investments, and fine-tune them to get the best financial output.

(b) Consider your classmates or workmates. Imagine you are the lecturer or boss. What is the most efficient and effective way to communicate with these people to get the best outcome?

8

HOW TO WRITE A GREAT RESUME, ACE YOUR INTERVIEW, AND KICK-START YOUR CAREER

"Don't settle for average. Bring your best to the moment. Then, whether it fails or succeeds, at least you know you gave all you had."

— ANGELA BASSETT

The first impression that a potential employer sees is your resume. For that reason, you need to always put your best foot forward. Spending time on your resume and doing it right is essential, as this carves the pathway to landing the interview.

RESUMES AND CVS WHAT'S THE DIFFERENCE?

Resumes and CVs (Curriculum Vitae) are often used interchangeably, but there are subtle differences depending on what country you are applying for work. (Indeed, 2021). Typically a resume in the US and a CV in the UK are very similar, a concise summary, usually 1-2 pages, tailored to the role you are applying for (an employment version). They include your relevant qualifications, professional work experiences, and any relevant skills. In the US, you may also be asked for an academic CV. This is a much longer document typically listing all your academic credentials and experiences, publications, and responsibilities. These are usually only requested for individuals seeking fellowships or high-level research positions in industry. In the UK, New Zealand, and most of Europe, it is usual to be asked for a CV (the shorter one). Australia, India, and South Africa use the terms resume and CV interchangeably to mean the same thing (both the shorter employment version). Canada resembles the US, with a resume being the shorter employment version and a CV being the more extended academic version. We will concentrate on the shorter 1-2 pager employment version. This will serve the majority of your needs. For the rest of this chapter, I will call it a resume.

CREATING YOUR RESUME

For the most part, many companies use an applicant tracking system (ATS), an automated program through which your resume is run. This program will then analyze the keywords within your resume and determine which job and role you would best be suited for. Suppose these keywords are in line with the job listing for which you have just applied. In that case, you may make it to the next stage of the recruitment process. Still, if the keywords in your resume do not align with the job posting, you will be removed from consideration. It is, therefore, vital that you craft your resume for the specific job that you are hoping to apply for.

Because your resume often runs through an automated program, it is important to use your words effectively. You may not necessarily need to waste words on pronouns and articles, so these can be avoided. In general, this is what your resume would need to include (Bradley, 2016):

- **Make a strong start.** You want to list a summary of all your best skills right at the top of your resume. Start strong with the skills directly related to the target role and work toward general and soft skills. This is the first thing recruiters will see, so ensure this paragraph shows your best side.

- **Show your results.** While it is great to know what your job duties entail and what you are expected to do, recruiters can search online for the job description of someone in your position. There is no need to mention these things in your resume. Instead, mention the results you have yielded in the company and how you achieved these results.

Tip: Be prepared to articulate what you personally delivered, not what your team delivered. What was your achievement?

- **Show your growth.** It is important to showcase what you did to grow in a company and earn a promotion. This tells recruiters that you bring this expertise, ideas, and experience to their company, and you have the potential to yield this type of growth at their organization too.

- **Showcase your networking abilities.** Be bold and show who you have met and who you have worked with on a professional level. By including this in your resume, you show recruiters that people of notable character find pleasure in working with you and that you are successful in working with people of excellent caliber. If these people want to work with you, a potential hiring manager must also want to work with you.

- **Exhibit your knowledge**. Do not be afraid to flex your brain muscle and demonstrate the industry knowledge that you have. Stay up-to-date with all news, insights, and developments within the industry, and be sure you can show it in your resume.

- **Use power words.** Use active language and power words such as orchestrated, achieved, strengthened, and managed. Your resume should exhibit the mental understanding you know you have.

The general format of your resume is that it starts with your personal information. It moves on to a summary of your skills. It has a list of your professional history, which will vary depending on relevance and how long you have been in the workforce. Next, your resume will have your education, and lastly, it will have additional certifications and skills that you have.

your
photo

NAME SURNAME
YOUR JOB POSITION

A few words about yourself. Lorem ipsum dolor sit amet, consectetur adipiscing elit, sed do eiusmod tempor incididunt ut labore et dolore magna aliqua. Ut enim ad minim veniam, quis nostrud exercitation ullamco laboris nisi ut aliquip ex ea commodo consequat. Duis aute irure dolor in reprehenderit in voluptate velit esse cillum.

CONTACT

Your Address St.
Your City, CA, 00000

youremail@youremail
youwebsite\links here

+0 000 000 0000

social network 1
social network 2
social network 3

LANGUAGES

Language (native)
● ● ● ● ● ● ● ● ●

Language (B2)
● ● ● ● ● ● ●

Language (B1)
● ● ● ● ●

SKILLS

A Very Good Skill
● ● ● ● ● ● ● ●

A Very Important Skill
● ● ● ● ● ● ● ●

A Very Important Skill
● ● ● ● ●

A Very Good Skill
● ● ● ● ● ● ●

A Very Important Skill
● ● ● ● ●

WORK EXPIRIENCE

2010 - 2017 LOREM IPSUM DOLOR SIT AMET
Lorem ipsum dolor sit amet, consectetur adipiscing elit, sed do eiusmod tempor incididunt ut labore et dolore magna aliqua.

2007 - 2010 IPSUM DOLOR SIT AMET
Velutpat blandit aliquam etiam erat velit scelerisque in dictum. Elementum sagittis vitae et leo duis ut diam quam nulla. Diam vel quam elementum pulvinar etiam non quam.

2006 - 2007 LOREM IPSUM DOLOR SIT AMET
Lorem ipsum dolor sit amet, consectetur adipiscing elit, sed do eiusmod tempor incididunt ut labore et dolore magna aliqua. Volutpat blandit.

EDUCATION

2007 - 2008 LOREM IPSUM DOLOR
Lorem ipsum dolor sit amet, consectetur adipiscing elit, sed do eiusmod tempor incididunt ut labore et dolore magna aliqua.

2002 - 2005 LOREM IPSUM DOLOR
Velutpat blandit aliquam etiam erat velit scelerisque in dictum. Elementum sagittis vitae et leo duis ut diam quam nulla. Diam vel quam elementum pulvinar etiam non quam.

ACHIEVEMENTS

2007 ACHIEVEMENT
Lorem ipsum dolor sit amet, consectetur adipiscing elit

2006 LOREM IPSUM SIT AMET
Lorem ipsum dolor sit amet, consectetur adipiscing elit

2005 LOREM IPSUM DOLOR
Lorem ipsum dolor sit amet, consectetur adipiscing elit

2005 IPSUM IPSUM IPSUM DOLOR SIT AMET
Lorem ipsum dolor sit amet, consectetur adipiscing elit

Suppose you are concerned about formatting errors that may arise in your resume. In that case, you could always use a template and find the appropriate guidelines regarding fonts, bullet points, and paragraphs. There are many free resume templates online. You only have to use your search engine to find them. Avoid the sponsored links at the top of the page, but look for the ones underneath. They are often higher up the web page and most utilized due to their quality and popularity. I recently discovered the resume templates on Canva.com. They are modern and have many different styles to choose from. Indeed.com (indeed.com/profile/resume-templates) also have excellent templates, so if you get stuck finding a template, you can start there.

Bullet important information so that it stands out and is easy to pinpoint. Your resume must remain consistent throughout, ensuring that it is in the same and correct format and has the same font and font size. The ideal length of your resume should be one page up to a maximum of two pages, depending on your experience and the role you are applying for.

IF YOU HAVE NO WORK EXPERIENCE

Suppose you are applying for your first job, which requires two years of working experience. You may feel deterred and unmotivated to apply for that particular role as you are fresh out of college.

However, you could boost your resume by listing:

- Your volunteer work experience
- Any part-time work you have completed
- Any other relevant experience

You might be surprised at how much experience you have once you list it. Show off your expertise!

Tip: Take action if you receive feedback that you still need more experience if this is a reoccurring issue of why you are not considered. Consider how you may gain the experience required, such as an internship at the same company or a more junior position than that to which you applied. We cover this further below: "getting your foot in the door!"

COVER LETTERS

A cover letter is sometimes optional and is used to further elaborate your skills and experience. The cover letter is adapted to the role you are applying for and will showcase precisely how your skills relate to the desired skills of the vacant position. You will tell the recruiter why you are the best person for the role. This is an opportunity to deviate from the standard resume format and allow your personality to shine.

Be honest and compelling. You may be the person they contact for an interview.

NAME SURNAME
YOUR JOB POSITION

Your Address St.
Your City, CA, 00000

youremail@youremail
yourwebsitelinks.here

+0.000.000.0000

DEAR SIR, MADAM

Dictum at tempor commodo ullamcorper a lacus. Tortor condimentum lacinia quis vel eros donec ac odio. Fringilla ut morbi tincidunt augue interdum velit euismod in pellentesque. Aliquet nec ullamcorper sit amet risus nullam eget felis. Viverra aliquet eget sit amet tellus. Volutpat blandit aliquam etiam erat velit scelerisque. Ac placerat vestibulum lectus mauris ultricies eros in. Enim eu turpis egestas pretium aenean.

Cursus eget nunc scelerisque viverra mauris. Nunc consequat interdum varius sit. Iaculis nunc sed augue lacus. Tristique senectus et netus et malesuada fames ac turpis egestas. Sed libero enim sed faucibus turpis in eu mi. Ultricies in iaculis nunc sed augue lacus viverra vitae congue. Diam ut venenatis tellus in metus.

Tellus cras adipiscing enim eu turpis. Elementum facilisis leo vel fringilla est ullamcorper eget nulla facilisi. Nibh praesent tristique magna ut amet purus gravida quis blandit. Laoreet sit amet cursus sit amet dictum sit amet. Massa tincidunt dui ut ornare.

Creative Art Director
Loremipsum Dolorsit Lorem Sitamet

Tip: It may be optional, but always add a cover letter if the process allows. You lose nothing by adding one. It shows you are serious about the position. If the recruiter is stuck between two people, it may come down to the one who bothered to add a cover letter.

Again if you are stuck on how to get started - Canva has free templates! (I should be on commission!)

GETTING A FOOT IN THE DOOR

Before preparing for an interview, know there are many ways to gain workforce exposure while in college or after graduating. The job you land may have been through a networking event, not because you sent your resume to a digital recruitment platform. Looking at other ways to find potential roles you could fulfill is essential.

The general expectation is that you will go to college, graduate, and head into the workforce. Still, sometimes the line from start to finish is challenging.

Be aware of networking events that may take place at your university or college. You can attend these while still enrolled at college or just after leaving. These events usually allow you to meet key industry players in a field directly related to your studies. Meeting these people will allow you the opportunity to make a great first impression and become someone to think about when the next job opening becomes available.

Aside from networking, it is never beneath you to work as a volunteer to gain experience. This is always beneficial when starting your career, regardless of whether you have worked. Volunteering is an excellent option if you are working toward a graduate or master's degree. If that best suits your desired career path.

You could also get an internship or an apprenticeship, significantly contributing to your work experience. Additionally, you could work as your own boss by trying to establish a passive income. Having a passive income is a fancy way of making your money work for you rather than you working for your money. There are a few ways to start a passive income.

This can be done by (Ferreira, 2021):

- Dropshipping (sell items without holding any stock)
- Monetizing a blog
- Selling items
- Posting sponsored posts on social media
- Renting out property that you own
- Having a print-on-demand store

Suppose you have design or marketing skills and the right software or equipment. In that case, you could try freelancing through Fiverr, and there are many other options.

It is essential to consider all your possible income streams rather than just limiting yourself to a job in the generic sense of the word.

Getting a job, whether small or large, temporary or permanent, provides you with character-building opportunities. Also, it allows you to obtain valuable skills that can't otherwise be taught, enabling you to experience what you do and don't enjoy doing.

INTERVIEWS

Going for an interview is a big deal. This is where the prospect of you getting this job becomes real. There are many ways to prepare and ace your interviews. It's more than just permanent and full-time jobs that will require an interview. You may be required to interview for an internship, an apprenticeship, and even volunteer work.

BEFORE THE INTERVIEW

RESEARCH

In advance, you will need to research the company with which you are having the interview and the people in the interview. This may be the recruiting manager, other senior-level employees, and the reporting manager for the vacant position. LinkedIn is a good site for this.

Tip: If you are applying for a role at a company you already work at, meet the recruiting manager personally before applying. It shows initiative and can put you higher on the list of potential candidates for an interview. Ensure you research the role as much as possible beforehand. From the moment you start working at the company, pay attention to the culture and dress code. Pay special attention to how management dresses. Is it casual and dressed down? Take a cue from them. You can do the same, keep it on the side of tidy and put together. You want people to think you are taking work seriously, not look like you have crawled out of bed and are still wearing pajamas. You never know when you will bump into the recruiting manager. First impressions can start a lot earlier than you know.

The same goes for pre-interview calls. Make sure you have done your research. These calls are often screening calls to thin the herd, so be ready. Not only will gaining intel tell you more about the company and the role, but it will also allow you to ask the interviewers appropriate questions. It allows you to be sure that the company is legitimate, honest, and fair. If you are applying for a financial role, ensure you know the financials for the business you are leaving and the company you are applying for. If you are applying for a commercial analyst role - show your commercial acumen. Suppose you are going for a marketing role; who are the company's competitors. What marketing campaigns are they known for, what is their brand, and what is their motto. If they sell or deliver a service or product, have you used it? Do your research. Even if you are going for an entry-level position - research what the company does. They are more likely to hire someone passionate, interested, and skilled than someone with just skills. So this is down to you - do your homework!

RESEARCH YOUR ONLINE PRESENCE

Once you have researched the company and role you are interested in, try researching yourself! Employers will do this before considering you for an interview. They will try search engines and check your social media comments, photos, groups, friends, and interests. How do you look to them? Don't underestimate this step! For example, employers don't want to see swearing, inappropriate nudity, reference to drug use, or any hostile behavior against minority groups. They will expect to see that you are an upstanding citizen, and if you have said you ride horses as a hobby, evidence of that would at least confirm there is truth in your resume. Use a common sense approach, clean up your accounts if you have to, and return to the start of when you opened your account. You can make accounts more private, but a recruiter did ask to become my friend on Facebook so they could check my account, so there is no hiding. You want to look professional online. An advocate for the new company you will work for. If you look like you will be good for their reputation, they will be more likely to hire you.

COMMON INTERVIEW QUESTIONS

Next, you will want to research some of the most common interview questions and practice your responses. Practicing should be easy because you are expected to be honest, so it will be easy to recall all true and correct information about yourself.

Here are some of the top interview questions that are asked and how you can prepare for them (Indeed Editorial Team, 2018):

1. Tell me about yourself.

> This is where you will tell them about your qualifications, why you applied for this role in particular, and why you would be a good fit for the company.

> Highlight your experience and background as it relates to similar positions.

2. How do you describe yourself?

> Here is where you can delve into your characteristics and your personality traits. You'd want to ensure that the qualities you choose to share are related to the skills and qualities required for the role.

3. What makes you unique?

> While this may be hard to answer, they want to know what will make you stand out. But you don't know the other candidates, so think of things that will benefit your employer if they hire you.

4. Why do you want to work here?

> Everyone wants to earn money to buy nice clothes or simply pay the rent, but that can't be your answer to this question.

> Instead, here is where you will showcase that you have researched the company, and you can use these aspects to state why you would want to join the company.

5. What motivates you?

> Here is the chance to be self-aware while allowing yourself to link personal and real-life stories and attributes to the job requirements.

Tip: If you have completed the career path exercise, you will already have some great input to draw upon.

6. What are you passionate about?

Employers want to know what drives you. They want to know that when they can't be your cheerleaders, what will get you out of bed each day and get you to work.

7. Why are you leaving your current job? (If you have one)

Be thoughtful in your answer. You don't want to make it seem that you are negatively portraying your former or current employer.

Still, you do want to maintain some form of honesty. If it is because of money, state so politely.

8. What are your greatest strengths?

Be sure to include a soft skill and a technical skill as it pertains to the target role and give them examples as evidence for why these are your greatest strengths.

Tip: Use your notes from the career path findings.

9. What are your greatest weaknesses?

No one wants to highlight their weaknesses or negative attributes. But suppose your greatest weakness is one of the primary functions of the role you are applying for. In that case, the company may choose not to proceed with your application.

Knowing your weaknesses shows self-awareness and willingness to learn and overcome such shortcomings.

Tip: Use your notes from the career path findings. When you get your results from any career aptitude tests, look at the areas where you didn't score highly. You could share one of these with the recruiter, but don't pick one vital for your role.

When you share a weakness, they expect you to explain how you are addressing it to make it a strength. If they don't ask, tell them anyway, it shows an excellent drive for self-development.

When heading to an interview, ensure you have read and understood the job description thoroughly and entirely. Prepare for your interview before time with a friend or a family member, and have a list of professional and character references that the company can call to verify you and your experience.

A **professional reference** is from someone who can vouch that you have the professional experience, strengths, and qualifications as stated on your resume. This can be a former employer, teacher, or someone from where you previously worked that knows you.

A **character (personal) reference** is from someone such as a teacher or mentor who can vouch for your character, strengths, and abilities.

SCENARIO-BASED QUESTIONS

They will also likely ask you four or five scenario-based questions that pertain to qualities needed for the role to which you are applying. These often link to your previous experiences and perhaps how you dealt with a difficult situation.

An example might be:

"In your previous role, give us an example of when you had to deal with a difficult customer or colleague and how you dealt with it."

If this is your first role, you only need to find a similar example of dealing with a difficult person, etc.; this may be someone at college, university, or in a voluntary workplace position. If they ask this question, they will want to see your conflict resolution and potential leadership skills and how you deal with pressure. Did you take responsibility for the situation or go get your boss? Before any interview, find some suitable honest examples.

They may also ask you scenario questions about sticking to deadlines or how you had to reprioritize your workload. Or there could be one to determine how you deal with pressure or when things go wrong.

STAR Technique

The standard format to structure your reply is by using the STAR technique:

- **Situation**. Briefly describe the scenario
- **Task** (or problem). Describe the issue or task
- **Action**. Explain what you did (not what the team did)
- **Result**. What was the outcome of your actions? Also, mention if you learned anything. Would you do anything differently?

Example of STAR in use:

QUESTION:

Give us an example of where you had to prioritise your workload in order to meet a deadline.

SITUATION:

I was asked to complete two different reports for two different senior managers at short notice. Both were due immediately. I had previously agreed to complete both when they requested it some time ago.

TASK:

I didn't know they would be required on the same day. Analysis was required on both, and a report was to be provided on each. I would not have time to complete both tasks in the time allocated.

ACTION:

I approached both managers to ascertain which was the most urgent and important. I also asked if it was a one-off report or if it is likely to be needed regularly. I reached out to a colleague who had the capacity to assist me, and I delegated the running of one of the report's analysis.

I prepared the outline of the reports for the managers. I discussed the findings of the analysis with my colleague. I entered the inputs and findings into the reports. I thanked my colleague and submitted the reports. I let the managers know it was a team effort giving due credit to my colleague and the team she came from.

RESULT:

Both reports were completed
satisfactorily and on time.

I learned I should have set expectations
with the managers upfront when
agreeing to accept the work and get a
better understanding of when the
reports would be due.

This isn't always possible with the ebbs
and flows of information requests, so I
saw the benefit of working further with
teams to share our pooled resources
when there is capacity, allowing us to
react quickly when information is
needed urgently.

The analysis in the report was also set
up as a query so it could be run much
quicker next time it was needed. The
managers advised that it would be
required again, but they didn't yet know
when.

This response using STAR lets us structure our answer in a concise and complete way. If you notice how I answered: I tried to show I could prioritize effectively while meeting deadlines as they asked, but I was also looking to demonstrate that I was reliable and results-driven, I can delegate effectively, and I work well with others to achieve company goals. I also wanted to show I could learn from my oversights and improve processes. There is a lot in this answer. It is loaded, and

I could have demonstrated more certainly on the prior-itization side, but it is just an example.

You need to practice a number of these before the interview.

Tip: They are not looking for someone who has never made a mistake. We are only human and, hopefully, learn from our experiences and mistakes. So they will be looking to see what you learned from your experience and what you did next time that particular problem occurred if, in fact, it did. Consider the role you will be applying for. What skills are important to do well in that role? They will tailor their questions to see if you can demonstrate that skill in the interview.

WHY ARE MANHOLE COVERS ROUND?

This was an interview question asked at Microsoft some years ago. It started a trend of brainteaser-style questions. I've not experienced one of these in a while - that was at a tech company where I applied to be a junior programmer. If given a brainteaser-style question, attempt your answer with positivity. You might have more than one answer. It may be a question with many answers or no correct answer, so simply keep your cool and have a go. It's better to have a shot at answering than saying, "I don't know," or "I would have to research that." These types of questions could be to test your solutions and analytical thinking skills, which might be relevant to the role to which you are applying. You may have to think outside the box.

So why are manhole covers round? There is more than one reason. The two main ones are if it is round, it won't fall down the hole, and a round cover is easier to fit. If it was square or rectangular, it would take more effort to line up. Can you think of any more reasons? That may be what Microsoft was looking for - fresh new thinking!

KNOW YOUR RESUME

After the recruiter has told you a little about the company, they often ask you to tell them about yourself. Nothing is worse than just reading pro rata from the sheet in front of you or even looking at it to prompt you to remember. It's best to have a fantastic sales pitch all about you in your head. You don't need to go into every detail but summarise when you worked there, what your role and responsibilities were, and most importantly, what you delivered personally.

Tip: Avoid saying, "*we* delivered this benefit." They don't get a measure of you. Instead, use "I delivered, executed, analyzed, evaluated..." - use power words.

Try to prepare at least one personal achievement for each role you discuss. If you haven't had a job before, draw on other experiences where you delivered or achieved something. Be positive and proud of these achievements and sell yourself. If it makes you feel better, the candidates most likely to get most roles do this. Nothing is worse than not getting a position because you didn't sufficiently prepare or give 100%.

TESTING

Some interviews have a test element. Not my personal favorite. You need to know your stuff. It's not always something you can revise beforehand.

Here are examples of some tests I have had to sit for different interviews.

- **Accounting Assistant**. A written test of my ability to perform double-entry bookkeeping that deals with certain transactions. Twenty questions, you either know it, or you don't.
- **Weapons Artificer - Royal Navy**. A basic entry exam with a range of questions on different topics. Nothing taxing if you are a grade C+ student at age 16. Then for the mechanical trade I chose - a written Math exam at least 1 hour in length - level equivalent to age 16, but

no calculator allowed. Then a written mechanical reasoning exam for at least 1 hour, with pictures of cogs and levers. Then during my interview, I was thrown an electrical plug and asked to wire it up. With the forces - Navy, Army & Air Force, you must pass a medical examination and ongoing fitness assessments while serving. Note: you need to have perfect eyesight to be a pilot. If you are tested colorblind, some aviation, engineering, and special ops roles will be unavailable - sorry if you were planning to be the next top gun.

- **Commissions Analyst (Telecoms)**. I was provided a laptop and asked to do data mining using their in-house data warehouse and Microsoft Access. I then had to analyze the data and present it back. If you are applying for a role that entails data extraction from specific systems, ensure you are familiar with those systems before any test.

- **Commercial Manager (Energy)**. I was provided a laptop and business case inputs. I was asked to find the profitability and discuss risks and opportunities. It was a real scenario that the business was dealing with.

- **MI5**. A timed Edward Glasser critical thinking test (approx 45 minutes). A lot of scenario-based questions with no spare time to think. The best time to sit these tests is when you have just studied for other exams and tests. Your brain will be optimally wired to deal with these types of questions. You need to be able to solve problems quickly. You can practice these types of questions. If you are serious about doing well, practice, practice, practice. This test is the first step in being considered. I sat with 100+ people in a room for the test. We left fifty minutes later, and another 100+ candidates entered to sit the same test. We will cover critical thinking in the next chapter!

So I will let you guess which roles I was successful with and which I was not.

Some online recruitment portals, such as Indeed.com, use skill tests. This is to help filter candidates for the recruiters. If you test well, you are halfway there! You have at least two options if you don't test well - like me.

1. Practice the requirements of the tests, and know your stuff! Then do the test. Ask yourself, are you qualified to do the role? If not, and it's what you want to do - take action.
2. Don't use that site; explore other channels and methods to apply for roles if you can.

Don't feel bad if you don't naturally test well. But in some professions, it may have more of a place, such as accounting or coding; you either know it or you don't.

But it's worth recognizing that this is a weakness for you and may be worth practicing or preparing for specific tests depending on your career choice. You don't want to miss out on your dream role because you may not pass a test, so recognize it as a gap or a weakness and look to improve on it.

Unskilled entry-level roles.

You have to use your head for these roles. There may not be a test per se, but they want to see you in action and may throw you in the deep end.

- **Bar and Restaurant Roles.** Research the company and the food and drink that the business sells. It is worth understanding food hygiene, and you can quickly get your own food hygiene certificate online at little cost. It takes less than half a day to complete and pass!. Having the right personality, customer-centricity, and enthusiasm will put you in good stead. They may get you to serve customers to see how you perform, but that's down to the individual employer. Some prefer you to have no previous training so they can train you themselves so it can boil down to your attitude and how you present yourself.

- **Manual Work (Laborer)**. Have the right attitude to take instruction, have common sense, and turn up on time. Can they work with you? Will you fit in well with their team? Have you had any similar experiences you can draw upon? If so, share this information with them. Have a can-do attitude. If they can use a laborer, they may put you to work to see how you get on.

PORTFOLIO OF PREVIOUS WORK

If the job requires it or if it adds value, have a portfolio of previous work ready for the recruiters to have a look at.

QUESTIONS TO ASK AT THE INTERVIEW

Prepare questions to ask those interviewing you, including questions not directly related to the position, you don't want too many, but your list could include questions like these:

> Why do you enjoy working for the company?

What would be the first project the successful candidate be working on?

What are the biggest challenges in the role?

What might a typical week look like?

How does the company measure success?

What development opportunities are there?

What is the culture like?

You want to demonstrate you are genuinely interested in the company and the role by asking questions. It's also a chance to show you have done your own research.

SALARY EXPECTATIONS

You can ask what the offered salary would be if it wasn't advertised.

Be prepared to discuss salary expectations, as awkward as that may seem. Do your research before the interview on what salary (basic and benefits) you would be willing to accept. Have an idea of the maximum and minimum salary for the position.

Tip: If this is your first role in your desired career, it can be worth setting your salary expectations at the lower range of what they are advertising (if the salary is not stated, research similar posts at other companies to understand the salary banding, look at glassdoor.com/salaries. Suppose your experience is zero or very little. In that case, the company will only be looking to offer you the lower end of the salary banding. This is, so they have room to increase it as you gain experience with them. The additional benefits package you could receive adds up and shouldn't be overlooked as you weigh what they offer. These benefits could include; healthcare, pension contributions, gym memberships, dental, and much more. If the experience you gain from working there is the primary objective or if it is the company you want to work for ultimately. Refrain from demanding a salary at the top of the bracket or banding. You can re-negotiate your salary a year or two when you are invaluable to them. This scenario works best when you are being promoted internally. Suppose you are experienced and know your skills are valuable to them. Your salary expectations could be anywhere within the advertised banding. Factors affecting the amount offered could be the number and quality of other applicants applying, so don't let it all be about money. Get your foot in the door first.

When preparing to accept a role at an energy company, I negotiated a 10% increase to the offered salary. This was due to the distance I would need to drive to work. Additional supporting factors were that I had the experience they were looking for gained from a similar industry (telecoms), and no other applicants were as close a match. You may not always be able to negotiate a higher salary, but it is possible in the right environment.

AT THE INTERVIEW

Finally, the day you have been preparing for has arrived. At the interview, it is time to put the preparation into practice.

- Choose and iron your clothes the night before. This will remove the stress of deciding what to wear. Remember to clean and polish your footwear if needed. If you need a haircut, also get this done. You need to look your best.
- On the day, if you need a shave, do so. Use deodorant; you may sweat more when nervous or running late. Don't wear overpowering fragrances. After showering, deodorant and a light spritz of fragrance are more than enough. If you wear make-up, less is more. Natural colors are safer.

- Carry extra copies of your resume with you, even though they may have a digital version of your resume, which you used to apply for the role.
- Take with you a notepad and pen. This can contain the questions you will ask and allows you to take notes when they tell you about the business.
- Be on time for the interview by arriving at least 5-10 minutes early. This will give an excellent first impression.
- Be polite and respectful.
- Smile often.
- When greeting, hold your stance firm, and have a firm handshake.
- Making eye contact when meeting and addressing people.
- Make an extra effort to remember everyone's name.
- Once seated, don't fidget or play with your hair or pen.
- If they offer you water, accept your mouth can get dry from talking, and excited nervousness can make you thirsty. You don't want a tickly throat or to start coughing.
- Don't cross your arms; it makes you look closed off and defensive. If you are nervous, place your

hands in your lap, relaxed but sitting straight with shoulders slightly back.

- Remember to make eye contact with whoever is addressing you. It builds rapport, makes you look prepared, and builds trust.
- Avoid looking around the room or at the ceiling for inspiration when asked a question. Experienced interviewers will know you are unprepared, or it could look like you are lying. It pays to be prepared.

This is when all your research and practice come into play.

- When asked, tell them about yourself, your experience, and your achievements without looking at your notes. Get eye contact. Keep your tone positive.
- Use STAR to answer any scenario-based questions.
- Have your questions ready for the end of the interview. This is usually at the end.
- At the end of the interview, thank them for their time, shake hands, and remember to keep it firm. Remember you are still being assessed as you walk through the building. They may walk you to the door and ask polite questions.

AFTER THE INTERVIEW

After the interview, feel free to send an email thanking the company for taking the time to interview you and consider you for the role. If a week has gone by and you have not heard back from the company, it is acceptable to send a follow-up email to find out if you are still being considered for the role. Unless they explicitly say that you should consider your application unsuccessful if you have yet to hear back from them within a specific time frame. When you are successful, you should hear back from them within a few days.

As much as you feel you deserve a role, you must fight for it! Don't assume anything. Where competition is high such as in a city for a trendy popular company, you need to bring your A-game.

To be successful, you ideally need the following:

- Put in the preparation
- Have the skills and education they are looking for
- Have the experience they require
- Be a personality fit
- Live locally or be willing to move

Basically, be the best candidate at that moment in time.

Being a personality fit is sometimes more evident in specific industries and even departments. Still, they are often clear in the type of person they are looking for in their job advertisements.

There may also be occasions when they already have someone in mind for a role. Still, always give your best. You may not get every role you apply for, but you may make an excellent impression for future positions. They may contact you if other posts become available. Learning from these failures is an invaluable skill to possess. Don't be afraid to fail. Don't purposely not prep but give it your best! Get feedback to learn, and see if you can close that gap - think of it as a feedback loop. That interview could be perfect practice to get you ready for the next!

Find the positive from your failures, and you will be a force to reckon with.

§◆

WHEN A COLLEAGUE OR COMPANY IS UNPROFESSIONAL

Some workplaces and companies are less professional than others. If you start somewhere and find that they are unprofessional and what seemed like fun jibes at first feels more like bullying, don't put up with it. Workplace bullying happens, and it can be discrete that you may not recognize it as bullying. If you suspect you are being bullied, understand the company's policy on bullying. If you can't stop the individuals yourself, try reporting it to someone more senior at the company. If there is a human resources department, you can inform them. If this is the company's culture, you are best leaving. Document everything, and keep copies of any emails or messages if relevant. Seek advice from citizens advice (UK) or consider getting legal advice, even if it is for a preliminary chat. Your mental health is paramount. Don't let these hiccups get you down. You will find somewhere better. You don't want to work in a toxic environment. You deserve the best.

9

SOLVE PROBLEMS LIKE A PRO AND INCREASE YOUR EMPLOYABILITY

"We cannot solve our problems with the same thinking we used when we created them"

— ALBERT EINSTEIN

One of the greatest leveling grounds in life is problems. Everyone has to face them and has their way of dealing with them. As you enter adulthood, you quickly learn that there are right and wrong ways to handle the problems that may arise.

One of the wrong ways is trying to avoid the problem entirely. Burying your head in the sand like an ostrich is no way to help. Being in debt is often an excellent example of this. Just because you can't see the problem doesn't make it go away. When faced with difficulties, the most important thing to do is address the issue head-on, not shy away from it, and actively seek out the root cause.

PROBLEM-SOLVING

You will inevitably reach a point where you must face a significant issue. It may be a project you are involved with at college, work, or personal life. It is best to step back and not make any irrational or rushed decisions. The best solution to any problem is to consider it over some time. So let's look at how you can deal with problems when they arrive.

IDENTIFY THE PROBLEM AND TRY TO FIND THE POSITIVE IN THE SITUATION.

Sometimes, identifying the problem is complex. For example, you create an app that fails one or many tests. The issue might not be the coding, as you followed your original process and blueprint to the letter. Perhaps the problem was the time of day you carried out the test. Did the test coincide with updates or data-heavy downloads, which made the app timeout? Or, since the app was created, has the test tablet been through an automatic update you were unaware of, making the app outdated and incompatible with the updated software? Identifying the root cause entails looking at all the data and information, including talking to everyone connected to the issue to get a complete picture and understand what is causing the problems you see. It's essential to do this with a positive attitude. A positive attitude doesn't necessarily mean looking for the "good" in the situation but instead staying optimistic that you can fix the problem. Interviewing people to ascertain why something may have failed will take diplomacy, no finger-pointing, blaming, or shaming. You need all the facts and truth to see the complete picture.

STAY FOCUSED ON THE ISSUE AT HAND.

If the issue is causing extreme emotions or anxiety, it can be challenging to focus on the problem. Try to focus on what matters and what can help you overcome the problem.

WHEN DEALING WITH PEOPLE, YOU NEED TO LISTEN ACTIVELY.

It's an integral part of problem-solving. Listen without interruption. Remember to be diplomatic. The intention is to get the complete picture - all the facts!

FIND MORE THAN ONE SOLUTION.

Remember that the first solution you try may not work best. Have a range and test one change or improvement at a time.

BEFORE IMPLEMENTING YOUR FIRST IMPROVEMENT, CONSIDER THE PROS AND CONS OF EACH OPTION.

There may be more than one option that will work. Does one option offer more benefits, or do you need to fix a single problem?

WHEN YOU HAVE YOUR CHOSEN SOLUTION, IMPLEMENT IT. DID IT WORK? TEST IT.

Remember only to test one change at a time to reduce the number of variables. If it didn't work, that's okay. Try another solution and repeat until resolved! You will do this by evaluating the result and being aware of people's responses to these solutions and outcomes.

SUPPOSE YOU ARE STUCK AT AN IMPASSE, WHETHER WRESTLING WITH YOUR MIND OR AGAINST THE OPINIONS OF OTHERS.

In that case, getting objective advice about the situation is best. Speak to someone you trust, someone with whom you can be entirely honest, and get their opinion on whether your approach to the problem may be viable. While you shouldn't make your decisions from a place of emotion, it is always best to share your feelings with someone you trust. It will allow them to rationalize why this problem creates these specific emotions within you.

Tip: A mentor at either college or work can prove immensely invaluable. When trying to grow as a person and professionally, their insight can be priceless, especially if they understand your particular niche or predicament. Getting a mentor can be as easy as approaching someone you admire and respect and asking them. You may be surprised to hear they are already mentoring someone else. The worst-case scenario is that they will decline. But they will be flattered that you approached them.

GAINING PERSPECTIVE

Some key factors may assist you in problem-solving. You can think aloud, which allows you to get out of your head and step back from the emotions and the mental processes that are operating with these problems. Allow time for these thoughts to grow and develop, and talk about the problem and the solution.

Sometimes when forced, solution creation can often evaporate. Our brains need some room to reset and see things anew. I used to sit in the British Library in

London to study. Outside the library on the forecourt was an art installation revealing the top places for idea generation. There was a model of a bathtub and a giant toilet! Have you ever sat on the throne at home and come up with a great idea? Or, while relaxing in the bath or taking a shower, you suddenly remember tasks you forgot to do or find you can create song lyrics? Why is this? Part of the reason is allowing your brain to wander and relax. Because you enjoy a bath or shower, your brain releases dopamine. The other part is the change of scenery and perspective.

Here is an example of perspective. On a team event at a company I worked for, we had to build a Playmobil structure of how we wanted our team to work - great company, right? Playmobil people and animals represented our team and other teams who worked with us. Once built, we all looked at it from each side of the table in turn together. Stood periodically on each side, we could see issues - not the same flaws and problems, different ones. Each viewpoint revealed issues from each Playmobil character's perspective. One Playmobil person looked left out and unsupported, and a wild animal represented another team! How was that the correct thing for us to do? It showed us that our ideal environment still had a long way to go. It still had many things that needed improvement in how we worked with others. We had modeled an 'us-and-them' rather than creating what makes us similar and cohesive as a wider team and, ultimately, as a company! When the CEO, who had joined us for the session, also looked at our prized team model, he saw even more issues due to his perspective as a senior director. So other people's fresh eyes can also add value and different perspectives. Just be prepared to be open to feedback and objective criticism. The biggest takeaway and eye-opener for me that day was that moving where we stood around the table allowed us to see more issues and solutions. It gave us a fresh perspective.

PROBLEM-SOLVING TOOLS

There are so many ways and methodologies that you can use to approach a problem and devise a viable solution. People have worked with a scientific sense of purpose to find the best way to solve a problem. And while there are so many ways, some methodologies prove to be more effective and straightforward than others.

PDCA

Plan Do, Check, Act (PDCA) is a well-known global model. The model provides structure to your approach to problems in a continuous improvement cycle when needed.

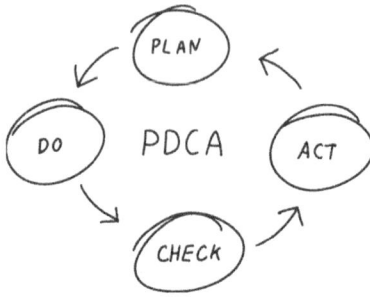

(P)lan: Define the problem. Collect relevant data. Perform root cause.

(D)o: Develop and then implement a solution. Gauge the measurement to determine if it was successful.

(C)heck: Compare before and after results.

(A)ct: Document the results. Inform others about process changes. Make recommendations for the next PDCA cycle.

Let's look at each stage in more detail.

(P)LAN

DEFINE THE PROBLEM

To define a problem, you must note the facts and be specific.

a) First, discuss with others, if necessary, why there is a problem.

b) Together, agree on the facts you know, not what you think. What, why, where, when, who, how, and how much are questions you need answers to. Write these down in a succinct summary called a Problem Statement.

c) Expand on any facts, capture when it happened, and any other factual observations.

d) Share the Problem Statement with relevant connected teams or someone close to the issue. Does the statement need any adjustments or additions?

e) Ensure that the facts are clear by defining any key terms.

COLLECT RELEVANT DATA

Now you have a clear, accurate Problem Statement. You can share this with other connected teams or people to gather more specific data.

Tip: In a large company, this is an important step. Suppose you get a department to offer personnel to help look into the problem. In that case, your approach needs to be efficient and professional. A clearly defined Problem Statement may allow other teams to quickly and accurately offer fresh perspectives, run specific reports, mine data and analyze, giving you insight and a complete picture.

Equipped with your Problem Statement, other data, and any new insight, move on to the root cause.

ROOT CAUSE

If you only focus on fixing the symptoms, you will never fix the problem. There are simple tools to help you identify the root cause. Two commonly used tools are "Ishikawa" (the Fishbone Diagram) and "5 Whys."

ISHIKAWA (THE FISHBONE DIAGRAM)

The Fishbone Diagram is excellent if your problem relates to a process or project with many elements. The diagram gives you a visual of the many moving parts. It allows the user to map the factual issues captured in the statement in a visual brainstorming way. The diagram has the problem identified on the right-hand side. On the left are headings that help us focus on any causes we mark down on the diagram.

The standard diagram has six generic headings:

- Environment
- Method
- Material
- People/manpower
- Machine
- Measurement

Fishbone Diagram

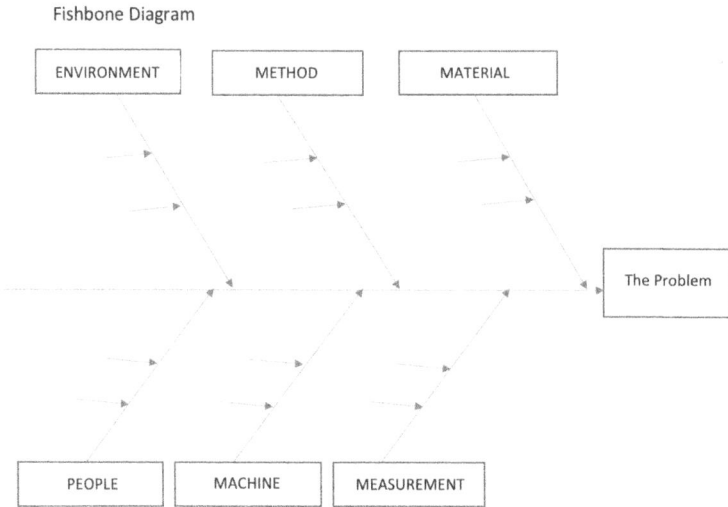

These work well for a production line with defects or issues in the manufacturing process. Depending on your problem, you could add other headings if they feel more relevant.

How to use the diagram:

1. On your diagram, write the issue on the right-hand side.
2. Add the category headings related to the cause (as above, people, machine, etc.) as branches off the central arrow.
3. Brainstorm the causes. You could do this as a group. Add the causes to the diagram as branches connected to the relevant category, i.e., "coding error by an employee," would go on

the People/manpower branch.

4. Once you have captured the causes, for each cause on the diagram, ask the question, "why did this happen?" and add those causes as sub-branches. Continue to ask why till you have explored all avenues.

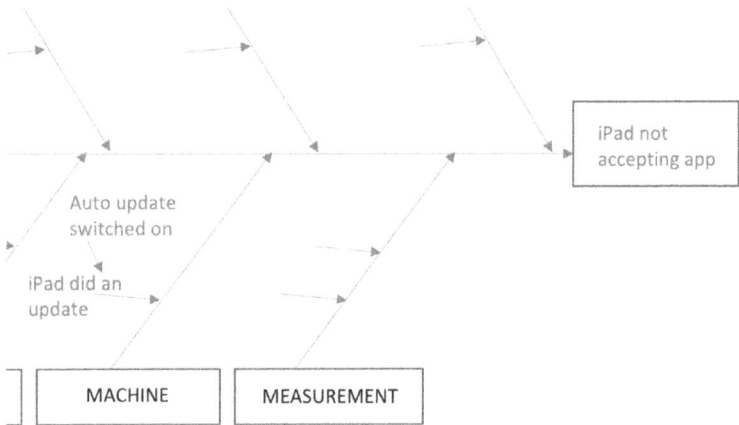

Auto update switched on

iPad did an update

MACHINE   MEASUREMENT

iPad not accepting app

Tips:

- Remember to focus on causes, not symptoms. 5 Whys (shown below)can be used together to get to the bottom of the causes.
- Give yourself enough space to add all your branches.
- You could draw a large diagram on a whiteboard or A1 paper if working as a group. The team can add the causes as post-it notes.

Once the exercise is complete, you can create a clean electronic copy for circulation. Also, take a photo of the live diagram and keep it on file, just in case.

5 Whys

5 Whys is the most simple of the models but helpful in actively getting you to dig deeper.

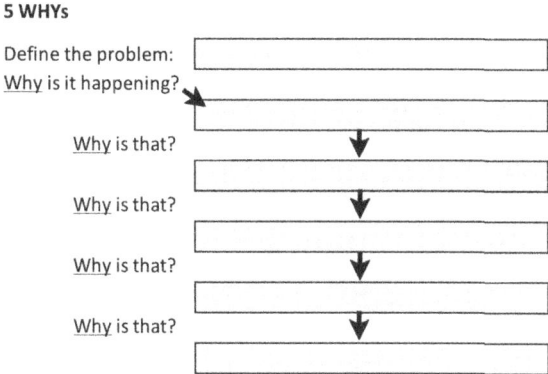

5 WHYs

Define the problem:
Why is it happening?

Why is that?

Why is that?

Why is that?

Why is that?

There is an excellent example I want to share with you of 5 Whys regarding the Thomas Jefferson Memorial in Washington, DC, USA.

The problem (in short): The building's stone exterior was deteriorating.

Why(1)? High-powered sprayers were used to clean it every two weeks.

Every two weeks seems excessive!

Why(2)? Why was it being cleaned so regularly with the sprayers?

It was cleaned so regularly because of excessive bird droppings on the building.

They thought they found the culprit and tried putting nets up, but that didn't stop the bird droppings, so they revisited the 5 Whys.

Why(3)? Why are there so many birds?

The birds were coming to feed on the spiders there. There were a lot of spiders.

Why(4)? Why were there so many spiders?

The spiders came to feed on the many insects there at night.

Why(5)? Why are there so many insects at night?

(IT SOUNDS LIKE A HORROR MOVIE!)

The insects were attracted to the bright lights that lit up the building at night!

So initially, they blamed the birds and focused on that with no lasting success. When in fact, the root cause was their own doing, attracting the insects at night with their bright lights. When they pushed further and asked more questions, they found the root cause.

So 5 Whys starts with the cause you are aware of and asks why. With each question, you hope to understand what may be causing the issue.

(D)o

Once you know the root cause/s, you can develop and implement solutions in this next stage. You may not be able to do this alone. It may be an issue for which you need assistance. You will need to decide upon a measurement to gauge if the change has been effective. You will then test using your solutions and measure the results.

(C)HECK

Then you will check and compare the results by looking at the outcome of the solution in a "before" and "after" type comparison. You can then determine if it was effective and whether your hypothesized result is accurate.

(A)CT

(a) Document the results: Lastly, you will note down the results of your process during the "act" stage, and you will ultimately have a solution for your problem by the end of the cycle.

(b) Inform others about the issue, steps taken, and process changes: Inform others so they can make any necessary adjustments to their processes. So they are aware of how to approach similar issues.

(c) Make recommendations for the next PDCA cycle: If the desired result is not achieved, make recommendations for the next cycle. Only make one change at a time. Changing many things in one cycle will likely give you too many variables, making it unclear what and why a test failed or is successful.

While PDCA takes a scientific approach to solving problems, you could use these methods as a practical daily way of solving and addressing personal issues.

Imagine you have insomnia. You can't sleep through the night without waking up, or it takes you hours to get to sleep! You would define the problem, gather necessary data, and use the Fishbone diagram and 5 Whys to capture and get to the bottom of all the causes. Develop and implement a change at a time. The desired result would be that you are sleeping through the night. You continue to make changes until you get to your desired outcome.

Some people only point out problems. Don't be that person. Equip yourself with the proper knowledge and skills. This skill becomes invaluable and sought-after when you enter the workplace. Approach problems by adding value - point out the problem and provide solutions by addressing the root cause.

DECISION MAKING

The mere fact that we are human means we can think for ourselves and make our own decisions. Understanding how and why we make certain decisions is integral to maturing and growing. We've been making decisions all our lives since we were babies. Through infancy and childhood, we made fewer decisions but made more and more as we got older, all of which contributed to our development. But making a decision is not just about choosing between two options. It's our thought process and understanding of the consequences of every decision. When you make an informed decision, you understand the implications and know which voice will likely have the best potential outcome. The reality is that our choices don't just affect us, but they affect others around us too.

So when we face our problems head-on, we need to know and understand what this exactly means to us and those around us.

There are strategies that you could and should follow when faced with significant decisions.

Whenever faced with making a decision that I am struggling with, I follow a few strategies that assist me in making the best decision. Given that our lives consist of many choices, making your decision-making process a good habit is always best.

When you make a decision, you first want to:

PROJECT YOURSELF SLIGHTLY INTO THE FUTURE.

You want to think about the different outcomes that each option may present, and you want to think about the immediate and long-term effects. Consider, for example, whether you should buy that extremely greasy burger for dinner or head home and make dinner yourself. The immediate outcome is the instant gratification that the burger will provide you, whereas cooking at home will take up too much time. The long-term result is that you will feel better after eating a home-cooked meal instead of bloated and uncomfortable after takeout. Next, you are going to:

COMPARE ALTERNATIVES.

Remember that the easier choice isn't always the best. Consider the negative results a decision may yield, and consider the risk of each decision. And lastly:

BE OPEN TO SUGGESTIONS.

The best choice or decision may be the one you have yet to hear.

BECOMING EMPLOYABLE

Everything you learn in school and every step you take culminates in an end state that is never truly your end state. You work hard in school, and then you work hard in college to reach a point where you are eligible for your first job. Then you get another job and another, and every time you prepare for a new one, you feel nervous all over again. But that is one of the best parts of being human—we constantly learn and evolve.

COMMUNICATION

To be employable, the essential skill you need to have is communication. Not only do you need to consider that people speak different languages and communicate in different ways, but personality differences also need to be taken into account. As some people are introverts, and others are extroverts. You also must consider and understand an individual's temperament before deciding the best way to communicate with them.

While talking may be the preferred way of communication for many people, for others, it can be anxiety-inducing. But luckily, other forms of communication are sometimes equally effective, and you should work on perfecting them. Writing and nonverbal cues play an important role in communication and have their place in business. You can also use different communication modes, such as telephone or email. The good thing about communication is as a skill, you have plenty of opportunities to practice. At the coffee shop, the mall (supermarket), talking to educators, talking to students you know, students you don't know. Have fun with it. You will be surprised how much you can improve with daily practice.

ACTIVE LISTENING

An essential aspect of communication is listening, which we often need help to do. We prefer to be heard and to make our opinions known. We appreciate being listened to properly. When you listen to someone, you need to genuinely listen and approach them from the point of empathy so that you can truly understand their perspective. This active listening helps mutual understanding, which is essential to resolve problems.

NEGOTIATING SKILLS

While negotiating skills may seem like you're trying to get the upper hand on someone, it is a great skill to have, especially when starting your first job. You can create a win-win situation because the company hiring you will employ a skilled employee, and you may negotiate a higher salary worth your expertise. Negotiating skills help build relationships and help avoid conflict. The goal is to find a compromise where both sides feel they have gained something positive from the situation. The idea is to find a mutually acceptable position compared to the original scenario where only one benefits. For this to work, both sides must be encouraged to move from their original position, which takes practice. Can you see and create win-win situations? Try practicing at home with family or friends.

LEADERSHIP SKILLS

It's worth mentioning that many of the skills covered so far in this book are vital skills needed in good leadership. There is an argument that some people are born leaders. Some believe it's in our DNA. Our early life experiences and influences may further prepare some of us at a younger age than others. Leadership can be learned, developed, and mastered regardless of your beliefs, DNA, or early childhood experiences. So what skills do you need to be a good leader? Let's see what we have already covered and fill in any gaps!

1. The ability to create goals and deliver them (in Chp. 4)
2. Excellent communication skills (included above)
3. Negotiation skills (included above)
4. Decision-making skills (included above)
5. Open to trying new things. It is keeping an open mind to new perspectives. You will never learn anything new if you only focus on old ideas and processes. Find people with new outlooks and ideas and reach out to them. Don't stay within your comfort zone. Push new boundaries and explore new ideas or you will never grow and develop. Be bold and brave!
6. The ability to work well with others:

- Build good working relationships from the start. Quality time helps, such as having lunch or a coffee together.
- Get to know the person, ask questions and take an interest.
- Be respectful. You won't get on with everyone. That's just life. But respect other people's views

and differences. It will help your working relationships.

- Less is more - don't overshare! Don't gossip. It doesn't create a professional, friendly environment. Avoid being constantly negative around colleagues. It will rub off on others like reverse empathy. Being positive will be noticed.
- Let new people feel welcome. Why not ask them to go for a coffee? It shows you are more team focussed than self-focused.
- Pull your weight! - Get your share of the work done. People may be counting on you.
- Be approachable - so if you want to progress to management, don't wear headphones in the office. You must be ready to chat with the team, not flying solo.
- Work with other teams if you get the chance. Working with other business areas will expand your knowledge and your friend group. It may also open more growth opportunities for you later.
- Workplace etiquette.
- Be on time.
- Dress for the job you want.
- Don't swear.
- Keep your voice down if having a conversation.
- Keep emails, and computer use professional.

- Have positive co-worker relationships. You can make great friendships at work, making the workplace more enjoyable and productive as you work together toward common goals.

Realize you may have many of the above skills already. They require you to recognize, fine-tune, practice, and focus on them. You are at the perfect age to start practicing. This bit is now down to you.

> NOTE:
>
> It's not advisable, but if you find yourself in a position where you are dating someone from the workplace, you must be 100% professional. It must not make anyone uncomfortable or affect your work; this is very important.
>
> At work, you must put work first. From an onlooker's perspective, it should look like you are not dating at all, except perhaps at lunchtime when you sit together.

FURTHERING YOUR EDUCATION

Learning continues after you find work. You may find yourself completing training courses at a new job, or you may even find yourself with a strong desire to pursue further study. Furthering your studies, skills, and training makes you more employable. You show potential employers that you are prepared to upskill, learn and grow. It makes you appealing because you are willing to be molded into the role. It gives you bonus points, especially when you consider hunting for a job is tricky.

Studying further doesn't just allow you to learn new things; it helps grow your interests, expand your perception, build your character, and become an effective problem-solver. You provide benefits not only to yourself but to future employers, too. Becoming an invaluable company member will secure your role and open doors to promotion. It also puts you in a favorable position if you decide to jump ship and join another company.

Continued learning poses many benefits. There is no reason why you should ignore this opportunity, now or in the future. For example: If you are interested in managerial roles in the future, taking a financial management course, i.e., Finance for non-Finance Managers or a financial qualification, will put you in great stead. At some point, managers are responsible for budgets and departmental performance, which will be valuable to you and look great on your resume. But you must be determined and driven to complete these while working full-time - bear that in mind.

When you enter the workforce, it is essential to approach your job and your duties with ethics and with integrity. If you need to learn how to do something, it is always good to use available resources to find your way. In all job positions, it is also essential to have a basic understanding of technology as so many roles operate in the digital space. However, you may need to gain specific skills. In that case, it is vital to show a willingness to learn and adapt as you enter new roles and work environments. You must also be open-minded and take constructive criticism with dignity and integrity.

As you enter a new job, it is always important to see every circumstance, good or bad, as an opportunity to learn and develop. Notice your flaws and mistakes, work on them, and constantly allow yourself to evolve into a better version of yourself. Remember that, while aiming to be an employable and valuable team member, getting the job or landing the role is only the beginning. It is the first part of your career journey. You should constantly strive to learn and develop yourself within the function. Just because you landed the job doesn't mean you should put in the minimum effort. Hard work is bound to reap the rewards later on.

10

DISCOVER YOUR CORE VALUES, WHO YOU ARE IN THE WORLD, AND HOW YOU CAN CONTRIBUTE?

"Ideas are a dime a dozen. People who put them into action are priceless."

— AUTHOR UNKNOWN

*I*t's good to know your underlying core values to understand what drives you. Holding up a mirror like this can also be an awakening, as this shows you how others see you.

DISCOVER YOUR CORE PERSONAL VALUES

Here are 20 examples of common personal values, but there are many more:

246 | ADULT LIFE SKILLS FOR OLDER TEENS

acceptance	compassion	generosity	selflessness
appreciation	courage	honesty	self-love
accountability	diligence	humility	spirituality
altruism	discipline	kindness	wisdom
brave	empathy	loyalty	tolerance

While there may be many ways to help you discover or create your core values. Try this as a kick-start to create yours:

1. Ask colleagues or teachers what it's like to work with you and whether they see or mention any values or strengths.
2. Find somewhere quiet to think. Make a list of people you admire. Write a few words about each person. What qualities, strengths, values, or actions do you admire about them? Use the list above if that helps. You will use this for inspiration.
3. Next, consider how you want the world to see you. Use the list above again if that helps, or you can add your own values.
4. Compile a list of 4 or 5 values that stand out as who you want to be and how you want the world to see you.
5. Put some meaning around it.

6. Add a short description in your own words for each value that helps you explain it in relation to you.

7. Describe how others benefit from each value.

8. Consider how these core values fit into your life, at college, with friends, family, and work. How can you apply them? Revisit this step periodically and think about situations you had to deal with. As time goes by, are you dealing with things differently? Are you growing as a person? We begin to glimpse our strengths and core values when tested and challenged in life.

Here is an example of one of my values. It may seem personal, but we are in this together, and it shows how honest and frank with ourselves we need to be.

Core value: Self-love

Description: I will respect, be kind and forgive myself. I love my uniqueness and embrace positivity.

Impact on others: I will lead by example. My children will learn to love what makes them unique through my model and the environment I create—looking at the world more positively. It also provides a concrete framework for healthy relationships at home, school, and work.

This value takes work. I am a reverse empath, so those around me feed off my energy and mood. So this value is vital to the well-being of those I work with and my family. It also gives me energy and positive mental well-being, a great way to feel at the start of the day, topped only for me with a good cup of coffee!

The aim here is to be purposeful in the world. But to do that, you may need to find what centers and grounds you first—perhaps accepting what you can't change, embracing your uniqueness, finding the good, and finding positivity. Once you do, you will be a stronger person for it.

Your values may change over time. You may discover that some are just a part of who you are and that you choose other new values to embrace. You may find values geared toward helping others rather than your-self. You may be acutely aware that you have greater access to opportunities than some of your peers. This realization may lead you to develop a strong value of wanting equality for those who are not as fortunate as you are. It takes someone genuinely self-aware to realize their privilege in society and consciously strive for the same accessibility for others. After all, that is what equality is.

WHO YOU ARE IN THE WORLD

Now it is time to get a bit introspective. As you grow and evolve into your own person and become more independent, you will take up more space, encounter more people, and ultimately venture out to find who you are and what you can do to contribute. During these moments of introspection, it is vital to think beyond yourself and broaden your horizons. Consider the world around you, who occupies this space, and how others contribute.

Remember, this is not a race. You are making your mark on the world at your own pace. If someone appears to be moving faster than you, that is great for them. Be happy for them, and allow yourself to follow your own timeline.

AN INTEREST BEYOND YOURSELF

Finding your place in this world and how you could contribute is tricky, especially when constantly surrounded by the idea that we need to put ourselves first. While it is true that you can't pour from an empty cup, you must get out of your mind and venture into the world. One way you can achieve that is by finding an interest beyond yourself. What are you passionate about that involves others rather than yourself?

- Do you love animals?
- Do you love teaching others?
- Do you love kids?
- Get involved in volunteer work, student clubs, and associations geared toward helping others.

These interests can make you feel more connected to people, the community, and life.

Empathy

Empathy, as an example, is vital on your journey toward finding your space in this world. Thinking beyond yourself requires you to have it. With empathy comes the unique aspect of viewing the world through a different lens and gaining a different perspective on what is occurring through the eyes and feelings of others. The thing about perspective is that we can all view one event differently. A culmination of every thought and influence we have ever had, and it influences everything we perceive. We view the world through a lens of our own identity. But having empathy and the ability to see things from another's point of view, acknowledging that these differences exist and that you can occupy a space with them in mutual harmony and respect, are significant steps toward thinking beyond yourself.

For this same reason, exposing yourself to different cultures, races, traditions, and religions are essential. It allows you to gain insight and access to different views and perceptions of others, breaking the illusion that only we and our opinion exists.

Once you understand and develop empathy, perspective, and the concept of differences within this world, you will be able to carry this into and throughout adulthood.

Diversity allows you to think beyond yourself in such a beautiful way that it will enable you to simultaneously fit in and stand out in the world.

The reality is that before you find your place in the world, you must first discover it. It is beautifully and intricately composed of differences. Knowing and appreciating these differences will allow you to find your space and let you blend and meld together with others to become the best version of yourself.

WHAT IS GLOBAL PERSPECTIVE?

Were we designed to be selfish? Whether for survival purposes that date back to the beginning of man or because so many facets of life have created us to focus on ourselves. We tend to view "ourselves" and "others."

But we realize how interconnected we are when we take on a global perspective. Through a global perspective, it is easy to see how your identity and the identities of others interact with each other. You notice differences and similarities and watch new cultures form and develop right before your eyes. You see, new cultures form through the marrying of two different cultures. A new generation with cultural truths different from yours can quickly start.

The global perspective allows you to see just how small the world is. How that different parts of the world can be so culturally and physically removed from each other but also intricately connected through politics, economic interests, and social interaction.

Gone are the days when we only had to worry about local problems. Global issues affect us daily. Social media and the internet also make the world even smaller. As a young person in this world, it is vital that you become globally-minded as soon as possible.

HOW TO BECOME GLOBALLY MINDED

Being globally minded may seem like a big ask, but there are things that you can do to broaden your mind and take on the world with a more global thought, looking at it through the lens of diversity. One way to become more globally minded is by traveling abroad and experiencing a faraway land. You may find yourself blown away by cultural differences. You can allow yourself to be utterly and completely immersed in them to expand your worldview.

You could even start smaller and venture into a different culture within your community. Try a new cuisine, experience prolonged interactions with others, and learn about their traditions. Through this, you will see what forces are at play in shaping society.

You may still need clarification on why developing a global perspective is so important. In addition to developing empathy and respect toward other cultures and societies, it allows you to see the real-world problems everyone on earth faces. Doing so will enable you to work together in formulating solutions to mitigate these challenges. The aim is not to understand the context of others but to actively walk in their shoes and understand how and why they live the way they do. This way, you are no longer trying to solve your problems; you are trying to solve global issues because you see how other cultures perceive these problems.

There are some issues where knowing your place in this world and having a global perspective will actively prove beneficial in working toward a common solution. These problems will not be solved solely by you or someone else single-handedly. Still, the total of small little acts from everyone is bound to change the entire trajectory of the world.

Some of the issues faced on a global scale are carbon emissions, greenhouse gases, human trafficking, and animal extinction, which leads to the loss of whole ecosystems. These issues are but a splash in the ocean of war, loss of life, and the more significant problems that are often too harsh even to mention.

What are the ways that we can work toward remedying these problems? These can be permaculture as an approach to land and settlement management; finding or developing alternative sources of energy; finding different farming methods; adopting and implementing the practice of reusing, repurposing, and recycling; purchasing locally sourced items; avoiding single-use plastics and packaging; and striving towards the reduction in the reliance of fossil fuels.

When you allow yourself the opportunity to step back and look at the bigger picture, it puts some of our daily problems into perspective. It makes us realize just how small they are. But it is important to remember that big changes start small, and they start with you.

SMALL CHANGES TO SAVE THE WORLD

What can you do to make a difference? Well, you need to know where to make a difference. There is no point in trying to solve a problem that doesn't exist. One of the biggest problems that we face on a global scale is that our planet is falling apart all around us. It is time we nurture and take care of it to restore it to its full health (World Wildlife Fund, 2017). You can do this by:

- **Using your voice.** Make sure that people know your stance toward practices harming our earth. Open discussions, ask people about recycling habits, and research how companies source their products. Sometimes, when you're trying to make a point, all you need to do is ask questions.
- **Be informed.** Nothing is worse than trying to appear passionate about something you know little about. Be informed. Knowledge is power. Learn the topic, especially if you feel strongly about it.
- **Exercise your right and your power to vote.** Elect people of influence that stand for the same hopes and changes that you stand for.

- **Reduce your waste.** Be careful of what you buy, and donate to causes that actively take the initiative to solve the problems the world faces.

If you would like to start smaller, there are other ways to save the planet and tips and tricks that you could use to make a small difference with a big and long-lasting effect (Guardian Staff, 2002):

- Use fabric to wrap your gifts instead of paper.
- Buy and maintain your own beehive (although this may not be feasible if you are allergic).
- Drive slower as this uses less fuel.
- Save water by taking faster showers. You can also get a shower water flow reducer or replace the showerhead with a water-saving one that limits the flow.
- Change your bulbs and appliances to energy-efficient models if you are able.
- Ride your bike instead of driving short distances.
- Buy local produce or start a herb, fruit, or vegetable garden.
- Consider repurposing throw-away items.
- Make use of recycling depots.
- Stop using single-use paper and plastics such as polystyrene cups.

Your small actions, combined with the billions of others across the globe enforcing and implementing these same tips and tricks, will undoubtedly create a significant, positive change for the world, and that is a global perspective.

AFTERWORD

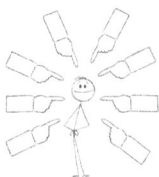

"If you want to believe in something, believe in yourself."

— KATIE WEBSDELL

So while I would love to teach you everything about adulthood that there is to learn, I can't take away the surprise of the inevitable joy of adulting. Trust me, it's not all about bills and working. When you grow into this role of being a responsible individual, the dynamics of those around you change. You will have a newfound respect and relationship that forms with your parents, and you will start developing meaningful relationships and interactions with friends you used to "hang out" with. Yes, you have a favorite parking spot at the mall (shops) and a favorite shop you buy your smoothie or latte from before work each day, but you also become a fully functioning member of society.

You may wonder how you will take care of yourself and the added responsibilities of having a car and paying your taxes on time while having a full-time job. Being an adult can be stressful, and being independent adds more pressure. But one thing that I can tell you is that it does get easier.

When you get into the rhythm of paying your annual car tax, performing your vehicle maintenance, and facing challenges and problems head-on, you will devise a personality that naturally approaches these situations with ease.

For example, once you get your first flat tire and change it by yourself, you won't mind being the person who volunteers to help your friend change their flat tire. You are then in a position to advise them about what next steps they should take and that they should head out immediately to have their tire repaired.

While it does get easier, the responsibility never fades. You get better at acknowledging it and dealing with it.

Now that you have reached the end of this book, I hope you have learned not just the joys of having your own car but also the responsibility it takes to keep and take care of this asset that you now own.

You also now know how to manage one of life's most valuable commodities: your finances. As tricky as this is, whether you are just beginning to gain financial independence or have been earning your own money for some time, finances are complex. If you grasp this concept effectively enough to manage your own money, you are well ahead of many in society. Allow me to let you in on a little secret. Many adults hire financial planners to help them manage their finances because they aren't very good at it.

Knowing how to take care of your car and drive it in all conditions will leave you the designated driver during the night, in the rain, and other weather conditions. You can carry this with pride as you are the person others trust with their lives.

Understanding how to uncover your career path and putting together a career plan with SMART goals will give you an advantage over many of your peers. It will allow you to see ahead with much more clarity. You now also know how to get organized and equip yourself with the tools, tips, and tricks to succeed in college and prepare yourself to enter the workforce. You have learned the skills to become a successful problem-solver and the skills to become an effective, authentic leader. By discovering your core personal values, you can shape who you want to be, find your place in the world, and share the knowledge you learn with others.

IN YOUR OWN TIME

It's never too late to change aspects of your life, whether you are a teen or an adult of any age; remember that! It could be a career or lifestyle change, or perhaps it's time for a mental or spiritual overhaul. If you can't do what you originally planned, work out why - make changes and make new plans. The tools and advice in this book are not just specific to teens; they work for adults too. There is no time limit on what you can achieve. So forgive yourself rather than give yourself a hard time if you feel you have let yourself down. Getting to know who you are - takes time and patience, and what we want as we get older changes too.

Never feel that you have been left behind if you see your peers striding ahead. Take it from someone who has been there. We can only do things at our own pace and on our own particular paths. If you have lost direction, you can remedy this - as I did. The information I have shared in this book and the first book, "Home Edition," will help you do that too.

AND FINALLY...

While I have discussed the importance of working hard and trying your best, if you constantly study or work hard, never taking time off, life will pass you by. Find the right balance for you! Well done to you for putting in the effort to become this person!

> "If you don't stop and look around once in a while, you could miss it."
>
> — FERRIS BUELLER

A LETTER FROM KATIE

Dear Reader,

Hey, you made it! Thank you for taking the time to read this book.

It does cover life skills in more detail than other books. The intention is to help you apply the knowledge more successfully. I also included extra resources, such as finding your career path and other sections, which are not deemed typical life skills but are vital to you as you begin to plan for your future. I wanted you to have a complete picture and feel armed and empowered!

As you made it this far, perhaps you would like to go a little further. To help me improve future editions of this book and help with future books in this series, I would really appreciate it if you could leave an honest review.

It only takes a minute - I always read them! Tell me what chapter or section you enjoyed the most or if it has helped you land your first job. That would be the cherry on top and make my day!

Wishing you the best adventures and success.

Katie x

KATIE WEBSDELL

ABOUT THE AUTHOR

Check out Katie's author profile on Amazon.

ALSO BY KATIE WEBSDELL

Adult Life Skills for Older Teens: Home Edition (Vol. 1)

Adult Life Skills for Older Teens: THE BIG ONE (Vol. 1 & 2)

BIBLIOGRAPHY

8 Financial Tips for Young Adults. (2022, May 15). Investopedia. https://www.investopedia.com/articles/younginvestors/08/eight-tips.asp

A. (2019a, January 27). *How Do I Check My Engine Oil without a Dipstick?* AutoAid. https://www.autoaidrescue.com/blog/how-do-i-check-my-engine-oil-without-a-dipstick-

Association of British Insurers. (n.d.). *Motor insurance.* https://www.abi.org.uk/products-and-issues/choosing-the-right-insurance/motor-insurance/

Advice Service. (n.d.). *Understanding your bank statement.* Reading University Students' Union. https://www.rusu.co.uk/pageassets/advice/money/Understanding-your-Bank-Statement-Oct-17-3.pdf

Automobile Association. (n.d.). *Which loan is best for you?.* https://www.theaa.com/loans/articles/6-types-of-loans

Automobile Association. (2020, February 5). *How to jump start a car in 8 steps.* https://www.theaa.com/breakdown-cover/advice/using-jump-leads

Bank of America. (n.d.). *What teens should know before buying a car.* https://bettermoneyhabits.bankofamerica.com/en/auto/first-car-for-teenager

Bankrx. (n.d.). *Black color line handdrawing as circle shape and arrow with word PDCA plan do check act on white background.* Shutterstock. https://www.shutterstock.com/image-vector/black-color-line-handdrawing-circle-shape-2103856505

Birt, J. (2019, December 12). *How To Improve Critical Thinking Skills at Work in 6 Steps.* Retrieved February 18, 2023, from https://www.indeed.com/career-advice/career-development/how-to-improve-critical-thinking

Borrelli, L. (2022). *Best car insurance for teens of October 2022.* Investopedia. https://www.investopedia.com/best-car-insurance-companies-for-teens-and-young-drivers-4788362#toc-guide-for-choosing-the-best-car-insurance-for-teens

Boumans, E. (2017, September 29). *Car taxation in EU and USA: A different kind of "green."* Global Fleet. https://www.globalfleet.com/fr/new-energies-taxation-and-legislation/europe-north-america/analysis/car-taxation-eu-and-usa

Bradley, S. A. (2016, October 18). *7 simple but effective ways to make your cv stand out.* Top Universities. https://www.topuniversities.com/blog/7-simple-effective-ways-make-your-cv-stand-out

Buying a used car - the ultimate checklist | RAC Drive. (n.d.). https://www.rac.co.uk/drive/advice/buying-and-selling-guides/buying-a-used-car/

C. (2022, December 9). *How to Choose a Career: 7 Ways to Narrow Your Options.* Coursera. https://www.coursera.org/articles/how-to-choose-a-career

CashASAP.co.uk. (2019). *10 financial tips for young adults.* https://cashasap.co.uk/blog/financial-tips-for-young-adults.html

Cheshire Fire and Rescue Service. (2017, September 27). *Driving in heavy rain or on flooded roads.* https://www.cheshirefire.gov.uk/public-safety/road-safety/driving-in-heavy-rain-or-on-flooded-roads

Cheshire Fire and Rescue Service. (2018, October 24). *Driving during high winds.* https://www.cheshirefire.gov.uk/public-safety/road-safety/driving-during-high-winds

Cheshire Fire and Rescue Service. (2019, May 9). *Young drivers - road safety advice.* https://www.cheshirefire.gov.uk/public-safety/road-safety/young-drivers/young-drivers-road-safety-advice

Choi, B. (2021, October 28). *How to use an ATM.* NerdWallet Canada https://www.nerdwallet.com/ca/banking/how-to-use-atm

Citizens Advice. (n.d.). *Getting a bank account.* https://www.citizensadvice.org.uk/debt-and-money/banking/getting-a-bank-account/#how_to_open_an_account

City of Chicago. (n.d.). *10 things every consumer should know about auto repair.* https://www.chicago.gov/city/en/depts/bacp/supp_info/10_thingd_every_consumershouldknowaboutautorepair.html

Cuesta College. (n.d.). *Decision-making and problem-solving.* https://www.cuesta.edu/student/resources/ssc/study_guides/critical_thinking/106_think_decisions.html

Dealerships, M. F. O. (n.d.). *What Documents Should I Get When Buying a Used Car? | Maguire Dealerships.* https://www.maguirecars.com/used-car-documents-ithaca-ny.htm

Dowleys. (2017). *5 things to look for when choosing a car service garage.* https://www.dowleys.co.uk/blog/5-things-to-look-for-when-choosing-a-car-service-garage/#

DrivingTests.org. (n.d.). *How to read a map of the road: 6 lifesaving tips.* https://driving-tests.org/beginner-drivers/reading-a-road-map-lost-art/

Enjuris Editor. (2018, November 21). *What to do if you hit a parked car [8 steps].* Enjuris. https://www.enjuris.com/blog/questions/hit-parked-car/

Equifax. (n.d.). *What is a credit report and what does it include?* https://www.equifax.com/personal/education/credit/report/what-is-a-credit-report-and-what-does-it-include/

Eva, A. L. (2018). Five ways to help teens think beyond themselves. *Greater Good Magazine.* https://greatergood.berkeley.edu/article/item/five_ways_to_help_teens_think_beyond_themselves

Experian. (n.d.). *How to improve your credit score.* https://www.experian.co.uk/consumer/guides/improve-credit-score.html

Ferreira, N. M. (2021, February 5). *21 passive income ideas to build wealth in 2021.* Oberlo. https://www.oberlo.co.uk/blog/passive-income

Get Schooled. (2022). *What teens should know about good debt & bad debt.* https://getschooled.com/article/5785-good-debt-vs-bad-debt/

Glassdoor Team. (2021). *How to write a cover letter.* https://www.glassdoor.co.uk/blog/guide/how-to-write-a-cover-letter/

Gobler, E. (2022). *Investing guide for teens (and parents).* The Balance. https://www.thebalancemoney.com/investing-guide-for-teens-and-parents-4588018

Gov.uk. (n.d.). *Vehicle tax rates.* Retrieved October 10, 2022, from https://www.gov.uk/vehicle-tax-rate-tables?step-by-step-nav=58fad183-27f5-4dd9-b51e-696c992373d7

Government Digital Service. (2011, November 16). *Legal obligations of drivers and riders.* GOV.UK. https://www.gov.uk/legal-obligations-drivers-riders

Grad Jobs. (n.d.). *5 reasons why you shouldn't stop learning after graduation.* https://www.gradjobs.co.uk/news-and-advice/5-reasons-why-you-shouldnt-stop-learning-after-graduation

Gray, S. (2022, July 16). Drivers urged to make extra check when driving in heatwave. *Daily Express.* https://www.express.co.uk/life-style/cars/1641161/driving-tips-heatwave-hot-weather-driver-warning-advice-latest

Guardian Staff. (2002, August 22). 50 easy ways to save the planet. *The Guardian.* https://www.theguardian.com/environment/2002/aug/22/worldsummit2002.earth21

Hailey, L. (2022, September 22). *Core Values List: The Only 216 Values You'll Ever Need.* Science of People. Retrieved February 18, 2023, from https://www.scienceofpeople.com/core-values/

Hansen, E. (2021, September 27). *4 ways to improve your credit score in under 30 days.* Upsolve. https://upsolve.org/learn/improve-credit-score-in-30-days/

Hitchman, D. (2019). *Six reasons why you should service your car.* Evans Halshaw. https://www.evanshalshaw.com/blog/6-reasons-why-you-should-service-your-car/

How the Federal Reserve Controls Inflation. (2022, October 24). The Balance. https://www.thebalancemoney.com/what-is-being-done-to-control-inflation-3306095

How to get credit for the first time | MoneyHelper. (n.d.). MaPS. https://www.moneyhelper.org.uk/en/everyday-money/credit-and-purchases/getting-credit-for-the-first-time

Immihelp. (2019, April 30). *Public transport in the USA, Tips for newcomers to the USA.* https://www.immihelp.com/public-transport-in-usa/

Indeed Editorial Team. (2018). *Top 16 common job interview questions and answers* Indeed.com. https://www.indeed.com/career-advice/interviewing/top-interview-questions-and-answers

Indeed Editorial Team. (2021, February 10). *10 ways to improve your analytical skills.* Indeed Career Guide. https://www.indeed.com/career-advice/career-development/improve-analytical-skills

Indeed Editorial Team. (2019, December 12). *10 Tips for How To Get Along With Coworkers.* Retrieved February 18, 2023, from https://www.indeed.com/career-advice/career-development/how-to-get-along-with-coworkers

Indeed Editorial Team. (2021, August 31). *Resume vs. CV: What are the differences?* Retrieved February 18, 2023, from https://uk.indeed.com/career-advice/cvs-cover-letters/resume-vs-cv

The Intern Group. (2017, January 24). *The growing importance of a global perspective.* https://www.theinterngroup.com/our-blog/what-is-a-global-perspective/

Investment Basics Explained With Types to Invest in. (2022, October 1). Investopedia. https://www.investopedia.com/terms/i/investment.asp

Jain, N. (2015, July 2). *What documents should I get when buying a used car?* AutoTrader. https://www.autotrader.co.uk/content/advice/what-paperwork-do-i-need-when-buying-a-used-car

The Jed Foundation. (n.d.). *Decision making 101.* https://jedfoundation.org/set-to-go/decision-making-101/

Lake, R. (2019, February 8). *What documents should you keep in your car?* Birchwood Credit. https://www.birchwoodcredit.com/blog/what-documents-should-you-keep-in-your-car/

Lavie, D. (2022, October 13). *How To Calculate Inflation: PCE & CPI.* Forbes Advisor. https://www.forbes.com/advisor/investing/how-to-calculate-inflation/

Lewis, M. (2018, July 2). *Student loans mythbusting.* Money Saving Expert. https://www.moneysavingexpert.com/students/student-loans-tuition-fees-changes/

M. (2019b, November 11). *How to Cultivate Leadership in Teens.* Middle Earth. Retrieved February 18, 2023, from https://middleearthnj.org/2019/11/11/how-to-cultivate-leadership-in-teens/

Mann (Silvermann), B. (2021, January 15). *How to read (and understand) your bank statement.* The Smart Investor. https://thesmartinvestor.com/banking/guides-banking/understand-bank-statement/

McGurran, B. (2021, November 19). *6 tips to avoid debt.* Experian. https://www.experian.com/blogs/ask-experian/tips-to-avoid-debt/

Metrohonda. (2023). *How to Fill Tires With Air.* Retrieved February 18, 2023, from https://www.mymetrohonda.com/how-to-fill-tires-with-air/

Mint Life. (2021, March 29). *Budgeting for teens: 14 tips for growing your money young.* https://mint.intuit.com/blog/budgeting/budgeting-for-teens/

Money Helper. (n.d.). *Direct debits and standing orders.* Money and Pensions Service. https://www.moneyhelper.org.uk/en/everyday-money/banking/direct-debits-and-standing-orders

Moneyshake. (2020, August 10). *How much is car insurance for a new driver?* https://www.moneyshake.com/car-finance-guides/new-driver-guide/how-much-is-car-insurance-for-a-new-driver

MoneySuperMarket. (n.d.). *Car insurance for new drivers.* https://www.moneysupermarket.com/car-insurance/new-drivers/

MyBnk. (n.d.). *Tip 3 understanding borrowing options.* https://www.mybnk.org/students/tip-3-understand-your-borrowing-options/

Popoola, N. (2017, July 17). *Eight reasons to regularly review your bank statement.* Punch Newspapers. https://punchng.com/eight-reasons-to-regularly-review-your-bank-statement/

Powerful Youth. (2020, May 13). *A beginner's guide to goal setting for teens.* https://powerfulyouth.com/beginners-guide-goal-setting-for-teens-smart-goals/

RAC. (2020). *How to change a tyre in 10 simple steps.* https://www.rac.co.uk/drive/advice/car-maintenance/how-to-change-a-tyre/

Randazzo, A. (2022, November 18). *Current Assumed Rate of Return for State Pensions.* Equable. https://equable.org/current-assumed-rate-of-return-for-state-pensions/

Reid, R. (2022). *Compare the market - I hit a parked car what should I do?* Compare the Market. https://www.comparethemarket.com/car-insurance/content/i-hit-a-parked-car-what-should-i-do/

Reifman, S. (n.d.). *Steve Reifman - 10 Reasons to Work Hard in School.* Retrieved February 18, 2023, from http://stevereifman.com/teach

ing-books/9-featured-articles/for-teachers/1-10-reasons-to-work-hard-in-school

RelocateUSA. (2016, August 26). *How to register a car in the United States.* https://relocateusa.com/how-to-register-a-car-in-the-united-states/

Rever. (n.d.). *PDCA cycle: A critical tool for driving any Kaizen process.* https://reverscore.com/learn-kaizen/continuous-improvemment-kaizen/pdca-cycle-driving-kaizen/

Rinkesh. (2017, December 24). *20+ extraordinary reasons why you should use public transport.* Conserve Energy Future. https://www.conserve-energy-future.com/extraordinary-reasons-you-should-use-public-transport.php

Rosamond, C. (2021, November 26). *Used car checklist: key points to look for when buying.* Auto Express. https://www.autoexpress.co.uk/car-news/used-car-guide/66420/used-car-checklist-what-to-look-for-when-buying-a-second-hand-car

ROSPA. (2017, November). *Road Safety Factsheet.* Retrieved February 18, 2023, from https://www.rospa.com/rospaweb/docs/advice-services/road-safety/drivers/20-mph-zone-factsheet.pdf

Gongala, S. (2022, September 27). *21 essential life skills for teens to learn.* Mom Junction. https://www.momjunction.com/articles/everyday-life-skills-your-teen-should-learn_0081859/

Shameer, M. (2015, February 6). *10 useful tips to help your teens solve their problems.* Mom Junction. https://www.momjunction.com/articles/help-your-teen-solve-her-problems_00326769/

Skhmot, N. (2017). *Using the PDCA cycle to support continuous improvement (Kaizen).* The Lean Way. https://theleanway.net/the-continuous-improvement-cycle-pdca

Steber, C. (2016). *13 signs you have street smarts & stay aware of your surroundings.* Bustle. https://www.bustle.com/articles/197864-13-signs-you-have-street-smarts-stay-aware-of-your-surroundings

Sutler-Cohen, S., PhD. (2021, December 8). *Core Values: What they are, why they matter, and how to define yours.* Medium. Retrieved February 18, 2023, from https://medium.com/@scoutcoaching/core-values-

what-they-are-why-they-matter-and-how-to-define-yours-
93164383eada

Tarpley, L. G. (2022). *6 ways to deposit cash into someone else's account.*
Business Insider. https://www.businessinsider.com/personal-
finance/how-to-deposit-money-someone-else-bank-account?r=
US&IR=T

Taxes in the USA. (n.d.). The American Dream. https://www.the-ameri
can-dream.com/taxes-in-the-usa/

Taylor, C. (2021). *How to ace a college class: 15 steps (with pictures).* Wiki-
How. https://www.wikihow.life/Ace-a-College-Class

Tsouvalas, B. (2020, November 30). *7 hacks for young drivers to get
cheaper car insurance.* Savvy. https://www.savvy.com.au/how-
young-drivers-can-get-cheaper-car-insurance/

UCL's Crime Prevention and Personal Safety Team (2020, December
3). 8 top tips to stay safe on public transport. University College
London. https://www.ucl.ac.uk/students/news/2020/dec/8-top-
tips-stay-safe-public-transport

What is inflation? (n.d.). Bank of England. https://www.bankofengland.
co.uk/explainers/what-is-inflation

White, A. (2020, August 16). *5 budgeting tips for college students that can
help set you up for financial success.* CNBC. https://www.cnbc.com/
select/budgeting-tips-for-college-students/

Woodbridge, M. (2022). *12 simple car checks to help prevent a breakdown
and keep you safe.* RAC https://www.rac.co.uk/drive/advice/know-
how/regular-car-checks/

World Wildlife Fund. (2017, December 7). *10 things you can do to help
save our planet.* https://www.wwf.org.uk/thingsyoucando

Zee Media Bureau. (2021). *Benefits of owning a moped.* Zee News.
https://zeenews.india.com/india/benefits-of-owning-a-moped-
2417553.html#

Image References

Barks. (n.d.). *Comparison graph illustration of compound interest and simple
interest.* Shutterstock. https://www.shutterstock.com/image-

vector/comparison-graph-illustration-compound-interest-simple-1927257878

Flat vectors. (n.d.). *Car driving tips and rules. How to jump start a car. Top view. Flat vector illustration template.*Shutterstock. https://www.shutterstock.com/image-vector/car-driving-tips-rules-how-jump-1283678278

forestgraphic. (n.d.-a). *CV / resume and cover letter template - elegant stylish design - beige color background vector.* Shutterstock. https://www.shutterstock.com/image-vector/cv-resume-cover-letter-template-elegant-784660930

garagestock. (n.d.). *Smart Goal Setting. Chart with keywords and icons. Sketch.* Shutterstock. https://www.shutterstock.com/image-vector/smart-goal-setting-chart-keywords-icons-374733466

Iconic Bestiary. (n.d.). *Monthly expenses planning checklist with receipts, wallet and calculator. Flat style vector icon illustration.* Shutterstock. https://www.shutterstock.com/image-vector/monthly-expenses-planning-checklist-receipts-wallet-443618578

junpiiiiiiiiiii. (n.d.). *red tool jack lift car for repair check Maintenance of cars.* Shutterstock. https://www.shutterstock.com/image-photo/red-tool-jack-lift-car-repair-1334472206

Kartinkin77. (n.d.). *modern brown leather men casual or business bag isolated on white background.* Shutterstock. https://www.shutterstock.com/image-photo/modern-brown-leather-men-casual-business-493282465

Kit8.net. (n.d.). *Plastic credit card and ATM machine vector illustration. Automated teller machine with cash flat style design. Cash withdrawal. Banking technology. Isolated on white background.* Shutterstock. https://www.shutterstock.com/image-vector/plastic-credit-card-atm-machine-vector-1949299987

inear_design. (n.d.). *hand vote at the auction, bid competition bidder, financial suggestion paddle, commercial market, thin line symbol on white background - editable stroke vector illustration eps10.* Shutterstock. https://www.shutterstock.com/image-vector/hand-vote-auction-bid-competition-bidder-1988242949

LongQuattro. (n.d.). *Black wind rose isolated on white.* Shutterstock.

https://www.shutterstock.com/image-vector/black-wind-rose-isolated-on-white-108640466

PainterMaster. (n.d.). *Checking and read oil dipstick in vehicle icon on white background. Vector icon.* Shutterstock. https://www.shutterstock.com/image-vector/checking-read-oil-dipstick-vehicle-icon-2079198784

Pankaj_Digari. (n.d.). *Vector Illustration of Engine Oil Inspection on a Car's Engine.* Shutterstock. https://www.shutterstock.com/image-vector/vector-illustration-engine-oil-inspection-on-1863114871

PeopleImages.com - Yuri A. (n.d.). *Never leave your drink alone. Closeup shot of a man drugging a womans drink in a nightclub.* Shutterstock. https://www.shutterstock.com/image-photo/never-leave-your-drink-alone-closeup-2147997771

RG-vc. (n.d.). *Modern plastic compass with scales and rulers isolated on white background. Contains clipping path.* Shutterstock. https://www.shutterstock.com/image-photo/modern-plastic-compass-scales-rulers-isolated-1242155920

udaix. (n.d.). *How to Change a Flat Tire infographic diagram with detailed conceptual drawing images step by step for driver educational awareness poster and traffic safety on the road concept.* Shutterstock. https://www.shutterstock.com/image-vector/how-change-flat-tire-infographic-diagram-630149213

VectorMine. (n.d.). *Iceberg illusion diagram, vector illustration. What people see and what is success hidden part of hard work, dedication, disappointment, good habits, sacrifice, failure and persistence. Life knowledge.* Shutterstock. https://www.shutterstock.com/image-vector/iceberg-illusion-diagram-vector-illustration-what-1627129384

Yuri Hoyda. (n.d.). *Silhouette of man in hoodie. Front back. Vector .* Shutterstock. https://www.shutterstock.com/image-vector/silhouette-man-hoodie-front-back-vector-780665749

Zdenek Sasek. (n.d.). *Cartoon stick man drawing conceptual illustration of team or group of six businessman doing typical office work.* (n.d.). Shutterstock. https://www.shutterstock.com/image-vector/cartoon-stick-man-drawing-conceptual-illustration-1071379244

Zdenek Sasek. (n.d.). *Cartoon stick drawing conceptual illustration of man or businessman sitting on small stack of coins.Business concept of wealth, savings and finance.* Shutterstock. https://www.shutterstock.com/ image-vector/cartoon-stick-drawing-conceptual-illustration-man-1166925436

Zdenek Sasek. (n.d.-b). *Vector cartoon stick figure drawing conceptual illustration of man or businessman seeding coin to ground or soil to plant money or banknote or bill flower. Concept of investment and success.* Shutterstock. https://www.shutterstock.com/image-vector/vector-cartoon-stick-figure-drawing-conceptual-1604016445

Zdenek Sasek. (n.d.-b). *Cartoon stick man drawing conceptual illustration of businessman breaking piggy bank with hammer. Business concept of economy and savings.* Shutterstock. https://www.shutterstock.com/ image-vector/cartoon-stick-man-drawing-conceptual-illustration-1048416883

Zdenek Sasek. (n.d.-d). *Vector cartoon stick figure drawing conceptual illustration of tired, unhappy,sad or stressed man or driver driving a car. Front view.* Shutterstock. https://www.shutterstock.com/image-vector/ vector-cartoon-stick-figure-drawing-conceptual-1608570592

Zdenek Sasek. (n.d.-c). *Vector cartoon stick figure drawing conceptual illustration of man driving car through swarm of bugs, flies, mosquito or insect.* Shutterstock. https://www.shutterstock.com/image-vector/ vector-cartoon-stick-figure-drawing-conceptual-1655840071

Zdenek Sasek. (n.d.-c). *Cartoon stick man drawing conceptual illustration of male worker or repairman with wrench and tool box or toolbox.* Shutterstock. https://www.shutterstock.com/image-vector/cartoon-stick-man-drawing-conceptual-illustration-1078366688

Zdenek Sasek. (n.d.-b). *Cartoon stick drawing illustration of man or boy riding the scooter.* Shutterstock. https://www.shutterstock.com/ image-vector/cartoon-stick-drawing-illustration-man-boy-1111747697

Zdenek Sasek. (n.d.-d). *Cartoon stick man drawing conceptual illustration of businessman who found easy and secure way through chaos of crisis.* Shutterstock. https://www.shutterstock.com/image-vector/ cartoon-stick-man-drawing-conceptual-illustration-784713733

Zdenek Sasek. (n.d.-e). *Cartoon stick man drawing conceptual illustration of graduate young man running up stairs or staircase. Concept of success, future and career.* Shutterstock. https://www.shutterstock.com/ image-vector/cartoon-stick-man-drawing-conceptual-illustration-1071379205

Zdenek Sasek. (n.d.-b). *Cartoon stick drawing conceptual illustration of two men or businessmen shaking hands or doing handshake. Business concept of cooperation or agreement.* Shutterstock. https://www.shutterstock. com/image-vector/cartoon-stick-drawing-conceptual-illustration-two-1204420762

Zdenek Sasek. (n.d.-l). *Vector cartoon stick figure drawing conceptual illustration of two men or businessmen beating problem with hammers, third man is going with bigger hammer. Concept of cracking or solving problem.* Shutterstock. https://www.shutterstock.com/image-vector/vector-cartoon-stick-figure-drawing-conceptual-1550325497

Zdenek Sasek. (n.d.-d). *Cartoon stick figure drawing conceptual illustration of man sitting behind office desk and trying to write something and thinking hard with pencil in mouth.* Shutterstock. https://www.shutter stock.com/image-vector/cartoon-stick-figure-drawing-concep tual-illustration-1386446693

Zdenek Sasek. (n.d.-g). *Cartoon stick man drawing conceptual illustration of father and daughter watching flowers and butterflies or nature together. Concept of parenting.* Shutterstock. https://www.shutterstock.com/ image-vector/cartoon-stick-man-drawing-conceptual-illustration-1096623803

Zdenek Sasek. (n.d.-j). *Sign hands pointing at successful Person or Individuality, vector cartoon stick figure or character illustration.* Shutterstock. https://www.shutterstock.com/image-vector/sign-hands-point ing-successful-person-individuality-2103836480

Zdenek Sasek. (n.d.-m). *Vector cartoon stick figure drawing conceptual illustration of smiling writer, man or businessman typing or working on computer. Empty speech bubble above him.* Shutterstock. https://www. shutterstock.com/image-vector/vector-cartoon-stick-figure-draw ing-conceptual-1469754617

Made in the USA
Las Vegas, NV
10 December 2023